AN
INTRODUCTORY
PORTUGUESE
GRAMMAR

AN INTRODUCTORY PORTUGUESE GRAMMAR

EDWIN B. WILLIAMS

DOVER PUBLICATIONS, INC.
NEW YORK

International Standard Book Number: 0-486-23278-6
Library of Congress Catalog Card Number: 75-31280

Manufactured in the United States of America
Dover Publications, Inc.
180 Varick Street
New York, N.Y. 10014

*The present edition is dedicated to
the memory of Edwin B. Williams*

Preface

The object of this book is to offer to the beginner the elements of the everyday language of Portugal and Brazil. Standard Portuguese is generally considered to be the language spoken in the region between and including Lisbon and Coimbra, but good Portuguese spoken in Brazil is equally worthy of the title. There are differences in pronunciation, vocabulary, idiom, and syntax, in intonation, velocity, and energy of speech. Brazilian Portuguese seems to be uttered more deliberately but less energetically. Some of these differences are too subtle to be the concern of the beginner, but the important differences in pronunciation, vocabulary, idiom, and syntax are noted in the appropriate places throughout the book. The word *Brazilian*, written in parentheses after a word or expression, indicates that the word or expression is a required or preferred Brazilian alternate.

The author has striven to keep himself free from the prejudices of puristic theory and the influences of Spanish usage. At the same time, realizing that Portuguese is sometimes taught by teachers of Spanish and studied by students of Spanish, he has pointed out some of the similarities and some of the differences between Spanish and Portuguese. Thus a knowledge of Spanish will become an aid instead of a handicap.

The book had to be written without benefit of frequency lists and an established body of syntactical doctrine. The author wishes to take this opportunity to point out the need for vocabulary, idiom, and syntax frequency counts and for more investigation, classification, and definition in the field of syntax in Portugal and Brazil, if continued improvement in the teaching of Portuguese in this country is to be assured.

The modern spelling, based on the Orthographic Accord between Portugal and Brazil, has been adopted with one or two exceptions (e.g., ãe for ãi; see section 20). A novel feature of the book is

iii

the simplified statement of the rules of stress (section 47) and the rules for the use of the written accent marks (section 48). As a further aid to the beginner in learning pronunciation, the stressed vowel of all stressed words is indicated throughout the paradigms, the vocabularies of the lessons, and the Portuguese-English vocabulary at the back of the book. This is done in the following manner: (a) in words requiring an accent mark (section 48), by the acute accent mark on i and u and on open a, e, and o, and by the circumflex accent mark on close a, e, and o, thus: í, ú, á, é, ó, â, ê, and ô; (b) in all other words, by a subscript point under i and u and under close a, e, and o, and by a subscript hook under open a, e, and o, thus: i̧, u̧, a̧, ȩ, o̧, a̧, ȩ, and o̧. In this way, the quality of all stressed a's, e's, and o's is also shown. All words containing x that occur in the book are found in section 45 with the pronunciation of the x indicated.

The author wishes to express his deep appreciation and gratitude to Sr. Camillo Camara and to Sra. Maria de Lourdes Sá Pereira for valuable aid in the preparation of the book and for reading the proof.

E. B. W.

Contents

CONTENTS

AN
INTRODUCTORY
PORTUGUESE
GRAMMAR

Pronunciation

1. The Portuguese alphabet.

LETTER	NAME	LETTER	NAME
a	á	n	éne
b	bê	o	ó
c	cê	p	pê
d	dê	q	quê
e	é	r	érre
f	éfe	s	ésse
g	gê	t	tê
h	agá	u	u
i	i	v	vê
j	jota	x	xis [1]
l	éle	z	zê
m	éme		

[1] Pronounced *sheesh*.

a) The letters of the alphabet are masculine, e.g., **o éfe maiúsculo** *the capital f*, **o tê minúsculo** *the small t*.

b) Although the digraphs **ch** (**cê agá**), **lh** (**éle agá**), and **nh** (**éne agá**) represent simple sounds, they have not been incorporated into the alphabet as their Spanish equivalents have. It is obvious that reference to **n** + consonant does not include **nh**.

2. Accented *a*. 1. Accented open **a** is pronounced like *a* in *father*. This is the sound of accented **a** except as noted in 2 below. Examples: **caso, parte.**

a) When followed by final 1 or by 1 + consonant, this **a** is pronounced farther back in the mouth. It is somewhat like *a* in *paltry*. Examples: **mal, falta.**

2. Accented close **a** is pronounced like *a* in *above* or *u* in *cut*. This is the sound of accented **a** when written with the sign ˜ called the til or when followed by **m, n,** or **nh**. Examples: **irmã, cama,**

1

a̦no, ba̦nho.   In Brazilian Portuguese this sound is still more close; it is somewhat like the sound of *e* in *met*.

a) When written with the til or when followed by **m** + consonant or **n** + consonant, accented **a** besides being close is nasalized. Examples: **irmã̦, ca̦mpo, a̦ntes.**

b) The accented **a** of the word **ca̦da** is close, although it is not written with the til or followed by **m, n,** or **nh.**

c) The **a** of the ending of the first plural preterit indicative of verbs of the first conjugation is an open **a** in spite of the following **m.** This is shown by the use of the acute accent.   Example: **falámos.**

3. Accented *e*.   1. Accented open **e** is pronounced like *e* in *met*. Examples: **se̦te, légua.**

a) Accented **e** followed by final **l** or by **l** + consonant always has this sound.   Examples: **pape̦l, re̦lva.**

2. Accented close **e** is pronounced like *e* in *they*.   Be sure to omit the sound of *y* which follows the *e* in *they*.   Examples: **me̦sa, mês.**

a) Accented **e** followed by **m** + consonant or by **n** + consonant is always close and is nasalized.   Examples: **se̦mpre, le̦nte.**

b) Accented close **e** before soft **g, j, ch, lh, nh,** or **x** in the region between and including Lisbon and Coimbra has the sound of Portuguese close **a** (section 2, 2).   In Brazilian Portuguese it is simply a close **e.**   Examples: **te̦nho, igre̦ja, coe̦lho.**

c) Accented **e** in final **-em** and **-ens** is a nasalized diphthong consisting of close **e** + *y* in Brazilian Portuguese; in the standard Portuguese of Portugal, Portuguese close **a** + *y*.   Besides indicating the nasal resonance, the **m** and **n** have no value.   Examples: **be̦m, ninguém, te̦ns.**

4. Accented *i*.   Accented **i** is pronounced like *i* in *machine*.   Examples: **i̦da, -íssimo.**

a) Before final **l** or **l** + consonant or before **u,** it has a similar but slightly more open sound.   Examples: **mi̦l, vi̦u.**

5. Accented *o*.   1. Accented open **o** is pronounced like *o* in *north*. Examples: **no̦ve, móvel.**

a) Accented **o** followed by **l** + consonant is open. Example: **vǫlta.**

2. Accented close **o** is pronounced like *o* in *note.* Examples: **tǫdo, bôca.**

a) Accented **o** followed by final **m,** by **m** + consonant, or by **n** + consonant is always close and is nasalized. Examples: **bǫm, rǫmpo, cǫnta.**

6. Accented *u*. Accented **u** is pronounced like *u* in *rule.* Examples: **crṳ, número.**

7. Unaccented *a*. 1. Unaccented open **a** is pronounced like *a* in *father.* This is the sound of unaccented **a** when it is followed by **l** + consonant, by **ct, cç,** or **pt,** by final **r,** and in a few isolated words where it is sometimes indicated by the grave accent. Note that the **c** of **ct** and **cç** and the **p** of **pt** are generally not sounded and have no other purpose in these words than to indicate the open vowel sound. Examples: **alguém, actǫr, acção, baptị̄smo, açúcar, pàdẹiro, àmanhã** (first **a**), **à** and **às** (preposition + article).

2. Unaccented close **a** is pronounced like *a* in *above* or *u* in *cut.* This is the sound of unaccented **a** except as noted in 1 above. Examples: **sabẹr, tẹrra.**

a) This is the sound of **a** in unaccented monosyllables. Examples: **mas, para** (both a's).

3. Unaccented **a** in final **-am** (used exclusively as an unaccented verb ending) is a nasalized diphthong consisting of Portuguese close **a** + *w.* Besides the nasal resonance, the **m** has no value. Examples: **fạlam, falạram.**

8. Unaccented *e*. 1. Unaccented **e** is generally pronounced like French so-called mute *e* and is often practically mute, particularly when final. Examples: **pedịr, conhẹce, frạse.** In Brazilian Portuguese this **e** when final is pronounced like *i* in *perish.*

a) This is the sound of **e** in unaccented monosyllables. Examples: **me, que, se.** However, in the conjunction **e** and the preposition **em, e** is pronounced like *i* in *machine* and with the nasal resonance in **em.** In Brazilian Portuguese, **e** in unaccented monosyllables is pronounced like *i* in *perish*.

b) When final and before an initial vowel of a following word, **e** has the sound of *y*. There is a tendency to elide the final **e**, if the initial vowel is unaccented.

2. Unaccented **e** followed by **m** + consonant or **n** + consonant is always close and is nasalized. Examples: **lembrạr, sentịr.**

3. Unaccented **e** is pronounced like *i* in *perish*, when it is followed by **s** + consonant, **x** + consonant, soft **g, j, ch, lh, nh, x** (= *sh*), or final **s.** Examples: **vestịr, explicạr, regẹr, desejạr, fechạr, melhọr, senhọr, mexẹr, ạntes, frạses.**

4. Unaccented **e** is pronounced like *i* in *machine*, when initial. Examples: **evitạr, eléctrico, exercício.**

a) It has the same sound nasalized in initial **em-** + consonant and **en-** + consonant. Examples: **empregạr, enviạr.**

5. Unaccented **e** is pronounced like accented open **e**, when followed by **cç** or final **l.** Examples: **direcção, amável.**

6. Unaccented **e** in final **-em** and **-ens** is a nasalized diphthong consisting of close **e** + *y* in Brazilian Portuguese; in the standard Portuguese of Portugal, Portuguese close **a** + *y*. Besides indicating the nasal resonance, the **m** and **n** have no value. Examples: **dẹvem, họmens.**

7. Unaccented **e** before or after another vowel is pronounced like *y*. Examples: **fêmea, pọ̃e, teạtro.**

9. Unaccented *i*.   1. Unaccented **i** is pronounced like *i* in *machine*. Examples: **dizẹr, iguạl.**

2. Unaccented **i** followed by a syllable containing an accented **i** is pronounced like French mute *e*. Examples: **difícil, visịta.**

3. Unaccented **i** before or after another vowel is pronounced like *y*. Examples: **dicionário, pại.**

10. Unaccented *o*.   1. Unaccented **o** is generally pronounced like *u* in *rule*. Examples: **dormịr, cạso.** In Brazilian Portuguese there is a tendency to pronounce this **o** as a close **o**.

a) This is the sound of o in unaccented monosyllables. Examples: o, os, por.

2. Unaccented o followed by m + consonant or n + consonant always has the sound of close o and is nasalized. Examples: lombriga, contar.

3. Unaccented o followed by l + consonant always has the sound of close o. Examples: soldado, voltar.

4. Unaccented o before another vowel is pronounced like *w*. Examples: magoado, moinho.

11. Unaccented u. 1. Unaccented u is pronounced like *u* in *rule.* Examples: mulher, unir.

2. Unaccented u before or after another vowel is pronounced like *w*. Examples: língua, quando, causa.

a) This sound in gue, gui, que, and qui must be shown by placing the dieresis on the u. Examples: cinqüenta, freqüente, argüir. Without the dieresis it is understood that the u is silent. Examples: guerra, quem.

12. Diphthongs. A diphthong is a combination in one syllable of a vowel and the consonantal sound of *y* or *w*. The latter are usually written i and u respectively but in some words e and o. And in some words they are not represented orthographically (see sections 3, 2 c, 7, 3, and 8, 6). The element *y* or *w* may come before or after the vowel.

Diphthongs may be accented or unaccented. When accented, the accented element is always the vowel; the other element must then have the sound of *y* or *w*. Thus in the combinations of i and u four diphthongs are possible: úi, iú, uí, and íu. In the first two, the unaccented element is *y*, in the second two, it is *w*.

13. The diphthong *ai*. 1. When accented, ai is a combination of open a + *y*. Examples: pai, saiba.

2. When unaccented ai, is a combination of close a (sound of *a* in *above* or *u* in *cut*) + *y*. Examples: pairar, saibamos.

14. The diphthong *ei*. 1. When accented, **ei** is (a) sometimes a combination of open **e** + *y*, always indicated by the acute accent on the **e**, and (b) sometimes a combination of close **e** + *y*, which is also pronounced like close **a** (*a* in *above* or *u* in *cut*) + *y* in the region between and including Lisbon and Coimbra.   Examples: (a) **hotéis, papéis**; (b) **coméis, leite, primeiro, cheio.**
    2. When unaccented, **ei** has the second of the sounds of accented **ei.**   Examples: **possíveis, faláveis.**

15. The diphthong *oi*.   The diphthong **oi** is (a) sometimes a combination of open **o** + *y*, always indicated by the acute accent on the **o,** and (b) sometimes a combination of close **o** + *y*.   Examples: (a) **espanhóis, dezóito**; (b) **oiro, oito.**   The second of these sounds (close **o** + *y*) is interchangeable with **ou** in some words (see section 18).

16. The diphthong *au*.   The diphthong **au,** accented and unaccented, is a combination of open **a** + *w*.   Examples: **mau, causal.**

17. The diphthong *eu*.   The diphthong **eu** is (a) sometimes a combination of open **e** + *w*, always indicated by the acute accent on the **e,** and (b) sometimes a combination of close **e** + *w*.   Examples: (a) **céu, chapéu**; (b) **aprendeu, meu.**

18. The digraph *ou*.   The digraph **ou** is not a diphthong in the standard pronunciation of Lisbon, where it has the sound of simple close **o**.   In some dialects, however, it is a combination of close **o** + *w*.   Examples: **outro, soube.**
    The digraph **ou** is interchanged with **oi** (close **o** + *y*) in most words, although **oi** is commoner and more colloquial; **oi** cannot be used in **sou** *I am*, **ou** *or*, the third singular preterit ending **-ou, outro,** and the preterits **coube, soube, trouxe,** and the tenses derived from them.

19. Final *-iu* and *-io*.   Final **-iu** is a combination of accented **i** + *w*.   Examples: **partiu, riu.**   Final **-io** is pronounced like final **-iu** or as a combination of accented **i** + *y* + **u.**   Examples: **pronuncio, tio, rio.**

20. Nasal diphthongs. There are three common nasal diphthongs: ão, ãe, and õe. As the second element of ão has the sound of *w* and the second element of ãe and õe has the sound of *y*, these diphthongs should be written ãu, ãi, and õi to conform with the corresponding oral diphthongs. However, only the spelling ãi has been prescribed for the *nova ortografia* (e.g., mãi, cãis), and its adoption has been slow and unenthusiastic. Until ãu and õi have also been sanctioned, it would seem preferable in the interest of uniformity to continue to use ãe. This has been done in this book, e.g., mãe, cães.

21. The diphthong ão. The diphthong ão, accented and unaccented, is a nasalized combination of close a (sound of *a* in *above* or *u* in *cut*) + *w*. Examples: estão, bênção. In Brazilian Portuguese, ão is a nasalized combination of the sound of *e* in *met* + *w* (see section 2, 2).

a) When this sound occurs in the unaccented position in verbs, it is spelled -am. Examples: falam, falaram.

22. The diphthong ãe. The diphthong ãe, accented and unaccented, is a nasalized combination of close a (sound of *a* in *above* or *u* in *cut*) + *y*. Examples: mãe, cães. In Brazilian Portuguese it is a nasalized combination of close e + *y*.

a) In the final position in some words, this sound is spelled -em (-en when followed by s). Examples: devem, homens, ninguém, tens. The sound is the same in -êm. Examples: têm, vêm (3d pl. forms). In teem and veem the nasal diphthong is doubled, that is, pronounced twice in succession.

23. The diphthong õe. The diphthong õe, accented and unaccented, is a nasalized combination of close o + *y*. Examples: põe, lições.

a) In põem this diphthong is followed by the sound of the diphthong ãe.

24. The nasal diphthong ui. The nasal diphthong ui occurs in only one word, viz., muito. It is a nasalized combination of u + *y* and is always written without the til.   Between the nasal diphthong and the t of muito a consonantal n is heard.

25. Nasalization.   All vowels that are marked with a til, viz., ˜ , that are followed by **m** + consonant or **n** + consonant, or that are followed by final **m,** are pronounced with a nasal resonance and are close.   Examples: **irmã, lembro, conta, comum.**   In addition to indicating nasal resonance, **m** and **n** sometimes have consonantal value (see sections 36, 1 and 37, 1).

Nasal resonance in diphthongs is indicated by a til on the vowel element of the diphthong, except in final **-am, -em,** and **-ens.** Nasal resonance is not indicated in the word **muito** (see section 24).

26. b.   **1.** In the initial position or preceded by a consonant except **s, b** is pronounced like English *b.*   Examples: **bastante, ambos.**

2. Between two vowels or preceded by a vowel and followed by **l** or **r, b** is pronounced similarly but without altogether closing the lips.   This sound is not as marked as the corresponding sound in Spanish.   Examples: **caber, sôbre.**

27. c.   **1.** Followed by **e** or **i, c** has a sound much like English *s* in *say.*   Examples: **certo, cinco, esquecer.**   This is the so-called soft sound of **c.**

2. Written with a cedilla, viz., **ç,** it has the same sound, that is, a sound much like English *s* in *say.*   Examples: **começar, aço.**

3. In all other cases, c has the sound of English *c* in *car.*   Examples: **ficar, comer, custar, crer.**   This is the so-called hard sound of **c.**

a) In **cç** and **ct, c** is generally silent.   Examples: **eléctrico, acto.** It is often used merely to indicate the open sound of a preceding unaccented **a** or **e.**   Examples: **acção, actual, direcção.**   This silent **c** is omitted in Brazil.   Examples: **ação, direção.**
28. ch.   This digraph is pronounced like *sh* in *shall.*   Examples: **achar, chover.**

29. d.   **1.** In the initial position or preceded by a consonant, **d** is pronounced like English *d.*   Examples: **dizer, mandar.**

2. Between two vowels or preceded by a vowel and followed by **r, d** has a sound somewhat like English *th* in *this*, although it is not nearly so marked a spirant. Examples: **nạda, pẹdra.**

30. *f.* The letter **f** is pronounced like English *f*. Examples: **fọme, defẹsa.**

31. *g.* 1. Followed by **e** or **i, g** has the sound of English *s* in *pleasure.* Examples: **gẹnte, giz.** This is the so-called soft sound of **g.**

2. In all other cases, **g** has the sound of English *g* in *go.* Examples: **gạto, lọgo, glória.** This is the so-called hard sound of **g.**

a) This is the sound of **g** in **gue** and **gui,** although the **u** is not pronounced. Examples: **guẹrra, guitạrra.**

32. *h.* This letter has no sound and no phonetic value except in the digraphs **ch, lh,** and **nh.** It is always initial. Examples: **havẹr, hotẹl.**

33. *j.* This letter has the sound of English *s* in *pleasure.* Examples: **janẹla, ajudạr.**

34. *l.* 1. When initial, between two vowels, or after a consonant, l is pronounced like English *l*. Examples: **leite, cavạlo, clạro.**

2. When final or followed by a consonant, l is pronounced farther back in the mouth with a sound somewhat like English *l* in *fault* and *old*. Examples: **mạl, rẹlva.**

35. *lh.* This digraph is pronounced somewhat like *li* in *filial* except that the l is pronounced with the mouth in the position to pronounce *y.* The sound is, therefore, a simple sound instead of two successive sounds. Examples: **ịlha, lhe.**

36. *m.* 1. When initial, between two vowels, or before **b** or **p, m** is pronounced as in English. Examples: **mạis, cạma, sọmbra, sẹmpre.**

a) In addition to having this consonantal value before **b** and **p**, **m** indicates a nasal resonance on the preceding vowel, which is accordingly close.

2. When final, **m** has no consonantal value but indicates a nasal resonance on the preceding vowel.   If the vowel is **a**, it has the sound of the nasal diphthong **ão** (section 21 a); if it is **e**, the sound of the nasal diphthong **-ãe** (section 22 a).   Examples: **falam, devem, fim, bom, comum.**

37. n.   1. When initial, between two vowels, or before **t** or **d**, **n** is pronounced as in English.   Examples: **nove, ano, dente, onda.**

a) In addition to having this consonantal value before **t** and **d**, **n** indicates a nasal resonance on the preceding vowel, which is accordingly close.

2. Before hard **c**, hard **g**, or **q**, **n** is pronounced like English *n* in *sing*.   Examples: **branco, bengala, longo, enque.**

a) In addition to having this consonantal value before hard **c**, hard **g**, and **q**, **n** indicates a nasal resonance on the preceding vowel, which is accordingly close.

3. Before soft **c**, **ch**, soft **g**, **j**, **f**, **l**, **r**, **s**, **v**, or **x**, **n** has no consonantal value but merely indicates a nasal resonance on the preceding vowel, which is accordingly close.   Examples: **pertencer, ancho, anjo, ênfase, honra, senso, convidar.**

38. nh.   This digraph is pronounced somewhat like *ni* in *onion* except that the **n** is pronounced with the mouth in the position to pronounce *y*.   The sound is, therefore, a simple sound instead of two successive sounds.   Examples: **banho, vinho.**

39. p.   The letter **p** is pronounced like English *p*.   Examples: **pé, mapa.**

40. q.   The letter **q** always has the sound of *c* in *car*.   It is always followed by **u**, which when pronounced has the sound of *w*.   Unless marked with the dieresis, this **u** is silent before **e** or **i**.   Examples: **quando, quem, cinqüenta.**

41. *r.* **1.** Between two vowels, before or after a consonant (except l and n), and in the final position, r is pronounced with a slight trill, which is produced by vibrating the tip of the tongue. Examples: cạro, brạnco, pạrte, lạrgo, falạr.

2. In the initial position and when written double, r is strongly rolled. Examples: rụa, cạrro.

3. Before and after l or n, r is stronger than the first of the above sounds and weaker than the second. Examples: Cạrlos, cạrne, mẹlro, họnra.

42. *s.* **1.** In the initial position, after a consonant, and when written double between two vowels, s has the sound of *s* in *say*. Examples: sentịr, pụlso, clạsse.

2. When single between two vowels and when in liaison before another syntactically related word beginning with a vowel sound, s has the sound of *z* in *zeal*. Examples: cọisa, os amịgos, nós estạmos.

3. Before hard c, soft c, f, p, q or t, in the same word or in a following syntactically related word, and when absolutely final, s is pronounced like *sh* in *shall*. Examples: escọla, estudạr, esquecẹr, os cães, nós contạmos. In Brazilian Portuguese (except in Rio de Janciro) this s commonly has the sound of *s* in *say*.

a) Before soft c or another s, this s is commonly silent. Examples: descẹr, os sapạtos. And before ch and x it is always silent. Example: as chạves.

4. Before b, d, hard g, l, m, n, r, or z in the same word or in a following syntactically related word, s is pronounced like *s* in *pleasure*. Examples: Lisbọa, dẹsde, rạsgo, mẹsmo, as mãos, nós desejạmos. In Brazilian Portuguese (except in Rio de Janeiro) this s commonly has the sound of *z* in *zeal*.

a) Before soft g and j, s is always silent. Example: as janẹlas.

43. *t.* The letter t is pronounced like English *t.* Examples: tọdo, até.

44. *v.* The letter v is pronounced like English *v.* Examples: vịda, lịvro.

45. x. When initial, before or after a consonant, and sometimes between two vowels, **x** has the sound of *sh* in *shall*. Examples: **xadrẹz, xịs, excursão, excelẹnte, Excelência, enxạme, bạixo.**

a) In initial **ex** + vowel, **x** has the sound of *z* in *zeal*. Examples: **examinạr, exẹmplo, exercício, êxito.** Note that in all these examples except **êxito**, the initial **e** of **ex** has the sound of *i* in *machine* (section 8, 4).

b) Between two vowels in some words, **x** has the voiceless sound of **ss** (English *s* in *say*). Examples: **próximo, trọuxe** (and all other forms of this tense and the derived tenses).

c) In a few words, **x** between two vowels has the sound of *ks*. Examples: **fịxo, táxi.**

46. z. Initial and between two vowels, **z** has the sound of *z* in *zeal*. Examples: **zêlo, fazẹr.**

a) This is also the sound of **z** in liaison before another syntactically related word beginning with a vowel sound. Examples: **lụz eléctrica, vọz agụda.**

b) Before hard **c**, soft **c, f, p, q, t,** or **s** in a following syntactically related word and when absolutely final, **z** is pronounced like *sh* in *shall*. Examples: **vọz passịva, uma vẹz.** In Brazilian Portuguese (except in Rio de Janeiro) this **z** commonly has the sound of *s* in *say*.

c) Before **b, d,** hard **g, l, m, n, r,** or another **z** in a following syntactically related word, **z** is pronounced like *s* in *pleasure*. Example: **a vọz do amịgo.** In Brazilian Portuguese (except in Rio de Janeiro) this **z** commonly has the sound of *z* in *zeal*.

47. Accent or stress. 1. Words ending in **-a, -as, -e, -es, -o, -os, -am, -em,** and **-ens** are stressed on the syllable next to the last. Examples: **mẹsa, mẹsas, lẹnte, lẹntes, lịvro, lịvros, fạlam, họmem, họmens.**

a) The syllable next to the last may be an immediately preceding **i** or **u**, which is, accordingly, stressed. Examples: **geografịa, continụas** (2d sg. pres. ind.), **gazụa, pronuncịe, continụe, gentịo, partịam, sorrịem** (3d pl. pres. ind. of **sorrir**), **continụem.**

b) If in a word with one of these endings, the syllable next to the last contains one of the digraphs ai, ęi, ǫi, au, ęu, ou, ui, and iu, the first of the two vowels of the digraph is stressed.   Examples: sąiba, cąia (pres. subj. of cair), lęite, męio, tǫiro, cąusa, dęusa, ǫutro, rųivo.   But if the digraph is followed by nd, mb, or nh, the second of the two vowels is stressed.   Examples: ainda, Coimbra, moinho.

c) If in a word with one of these endings, the syllable next to the last contains one of the digraphs ia, io, and ua, the second of the two vowels of the digraph is stressed.   Examples: diąbo, miǫlo, quątro.

2. Words ending in one of the digraphs -ai, -ęi, -au, -ęu, -ou, -ui, -iu, -ão, -ãe, and -õe, whether followed by s or not, are stressed on the first of the two vowels of the digraph.[1]   Examples: recąi, metąis, falęi, comęis (2d pl. pres. ind.), degrąu, judęu, falǫu, construi, azuis, partiu, irmão, irmãos, alemães, compõe, lições.

a) If the digraph is followed by final l, r, or z, the stress falls on the second vowel.   Examples: paųl, cair, juiz.

3. Words ending in -i, -is, -u, -us, -im, -ins, -um, -uns, -ã, -ãs, -l, -r, and -z are stressed on the last syllable.   Examples: aprendi, aqui, partis (2d pl. pres. ind.), Paris (city), indų, compųs (1st sg. pret. ind. of compǫr), jardim, jardins, algųm, algųns, irmã, irmãs, espanhǫl, faląr, senhǫr, rapąz, feliz.

48. Accent marks.   1. There are two accent marks, an acute and a circumflex.   As stressed i and u do not vary in quality, only the acute accent mark is used on them.   But as stressed a, e, and o have two distinct qualities each, the acute accent mark is used when they are open and the circumflex when they are close.   In other words, whenever an accent mark is necessary on stressed a, e, and o, that mark must be used which corresponds to the quality of the vowel, the acute for open a, e, and o and the circumflex for close a, e, and o.

2. Words not stressed according to the principles set forth in section 47 must bear a written accent mark on the stressed vowel.

---

[1] The same rule applies to the digraphs ia, ie, io, ua, ue, and uo (section 47, 1 a).

a) Examples of words not stressed according to section 47, 1:
falará, falarás, maré, francês, avó, avô, ninguém,[1] **armazéns.**[1]

b) Examples of words not stressed according to section 47, 1 a:
importância, família, literário, mútuo, água.

c) Examples of words not stressed according to section 47, 1 b:
saída, saía, deísta, doído, saúde, juízo, ruína, miúdo, viúvo.

d) Examples of words not stressed according to section 47, 1 c:
díada, Calíope, gloríola.

e) There are two types of words that are not stressed according to section 47, 2: (a) those that are stressed on the syllable preceding the digraph and (b) those that are stressed on the second vowel of the digraph.   Examples: (a) **faláveis, fáceis, bênção, órgão;** (b) **aí, país, baú.**

f) Examples of words not stressed according to section 47, 3: **táxi, quási, lápis, tríbu, vírus, órfã, órfãs, móvel, cônsul, açúcar.**

g) As no provision is made in section 47 for words stressed on the third from the last syllable, such words must obviously be among those which bear a written accent mark.   Examples: **alfândega, oráculo, pélago, pêssego, falaríamos, aprendêssemos.**

3. The acute and circumflex accent marks are required on **a, e,** and **o** in some words where they are not needed to indicate stress.

a) The circumflex accent mark is required on stressed close **e** and **o** in some words stressed on the syllable next to the last in order that these words may be distinguished in writing from similarly spelled words having open **e** or open **o.**   Examples: **lêste** (2d sg. pret. ind. of **ler,** to be distinguished from **lęste** *East*); **dêste** (**de** + demonstrative, to be distinguished from **dęste,** 2d sg. pret. ind. of **dar**); **almôço** (noun, to be distinguished from **almǫço,** 1st sg. pres. ind. of **almoçar**); **sêca** (fem. of adj., to be distinguished from **sęca,** 3d sg. pres. ind. of **secar**).

The circumflex accent mark *may* be used for didactic purposes on stressed close **e** and **o** in any word stressed on the syllable next to the last, even if no discrimination is necessary.   Accordingly, in this

[1] The use of the acute accent mark (instead of the circumflex) on final **-em** and **-ens** in oxytonic polysyllables is based on the pronunciation of the standard Portuguese of Portugal (see section 3, 2 c).

book, the masculine forms of the demonstrative pronouns and of the third person stressed personal pronouns along with their combinations with de and em are all written with the circumflex accent mark (see sections 66, 68, 96, and 97 for lists).

b) The acute accent mark is required on e and o in the stressed diphthongs ẹi, ọi, and ẹu in order to distinguish them from the stressed diphthongs ẹi, ọi, and ẹu. Examples: platéia, hotéis, papéis, herói, espanhóis, combóio, dezóito, ilhéu, chapéus.

c) The acute or circumflex accent mark (according as the vowel is open or close) is required on stressed monosyllables in -a, -as, -e, -es, -o, and -os. Examples: má, más, sé, sés, dê, dês, mês, pó, pós, pôs. On other monosyllables with close e and close o, the circumflex accent mark is used for purposes of distinction. Examples: fêz (3d sg. pret. ind. of fazer, to be distinguished from fẹz noun); pôr (inf. to be distinguished from por preposition); côr (*color*, to be distinguished from cọr in de cọr *by heart*); têm (3d pl. pres. ind. of ter, to be distinguished from tem, 3d sg. pres. ind. of ter).

4. The grave accent mark is used to replace the acute accent mark to indicate the open quality of the vowel in adjectives transformed into adverbs by the addition of the ending -mẹnte. Examples: fàcilmẹnte (from fácil), sòmẹnte (from só).

a) The grave accent mark may be used for didactic purposes to indicate the open quality of a pretonic vowel: Examples: àmanhã, pàdẹiro, frèguês.

The grave accent mark is used on the combinations of the preposition a with the forms of the feminine article in accordance with the open sound of the contracted vowel. These combinations are à and às.

Lesson I

49. Gender. There are only two genders in Portuguese: masculine and feminine. Nouns ending in **-o** (or **-u**) are generally masculine; nouns ending in **-a** are generally feminine. Most other endings are not sure indices of gender.

> **livro** (masculine) *book*   **casa** (feminine) *house*
> **céu** (masculine) *sky, heaven*

50. Definite article. The singular forms of the definite article are **o** (masculine) and **a** (feminine).

> **o livro** *the book*   **a casa** *the house*

These forms combine with the preposition **de** as follows.

> **de + o: do**   **de + a: da**

51. Indefinite article. The forms of the indefinite article are **um** (masculine) and **uma** (feminine).

> **um livro** *a book*   **uma casa** *a house*

These forms combine with the preposition **de** as follows.

> **de + um: dum**   **de + uma: duma**

52. Present indicative. There are three forms of the present indicative in English, e.g., *I speak, I am speaking, I do speak.* These three forms are all represented in Portuguese by the simple form **falo.** And this simple form is also used to ask questions: **falo?** *do I speak?*

> **falo**   *I speak, am speaking, do speak; do I speak?*
> **fala**   *(he, she, it) speaks, is speaking, does speak*
> **falamos**   *we speak, are speaking, do speak*
> **falam**   *(they) speak, are speaking, do speak*

53. Negative. In order to form a negative sentence, **não** *not* is placed before the verb.

> **Não falo.**   *I do not speak.*

16

VOCABULARY

bem well
a casa the house
de of, from, by
e and
falar to speak
o hotel the hotel
inglês English
a janela the window
João John

o livro the book
muito very
não no, not
o nome the name
a porta the door
português Portuguese
sim yes
também also, too

EXERCISES

A. *Translate the English words to complete the phrase or sentence.*
1. O nome *of the* hotel. 2. Uma janela *of a* casa. 3. *We speak* português. 4. João não *speaks* inglês. 5. Falo *English.* 6. *They speak* inglês e português.

B. *Translate.* 1. O nome do livro. 2. A porta da casa. 3. A janela do hotel. 4. O nome dum hotel. 5. Uma janela duma casa.

C. *Translate.* 1. Falo inglês. 2. Falamos português bem. 3. João fala português? 4. Não fala (he does not speak it). 5. Falam inglês? 6. Sim, falam. 7. Falamos inglês e português. 8. João fala inglês muito bem. 9. Não falamos bem o inglês. 10. Não falo português. 11. João fala inglês. 12. Fala português também.

D. *Translate.* 1. The door of a house. 2. A name of a book. 3. The window of the hotel. 4. They speak Portuguese. 5. We speak English. 6. John does not speak Portuguese. 7. I speak English very well. 8. We do not speak Portuguese well. 9. They speak Portuguese and English. 10. He speaks Portuguese well. 11. He speaks English too.

Lesson II

54. Formation of plural. Nouns ending in a vowel sound or diphthong. 1. Nouns ending in a vowel (oral or nasal) form their plural by adding -s.

livro	book	livros	books
casa	house	casas	houses
lente	professor	lentes	professors
irmã	sister	irmãs	sisters

2. Nouns ending in **-m** (which is not pronounced but is used to show the nasal quality of the preceding vowel) form their plural by changing this **m** to **n** and adding **-s**.

homem	man	homens	men
jardim	garden	jardins	gardens
som	sound	sons	sounds

3. Nouns ending in the nasal diphthong **-ão** form their plural by adding **-s** or by changing **-ão** to **-ões** or **-ães**.

irmão	brother	irmãos	brothers
lição	lesson	lições	lessons
cão	dog	cães	dogs

Which of these formations is correct for a given noun may often be determined by referring to the corresponding Spanish plural, e.g., for the above nouns: **hermanos, lecciones,** and **canes.** But note that the plural of **verão** *summer* is **verões**; cf. Spanish **veranos.**

55. Definite article (continued). The plural forms of the definite article are **os** (masculine) and **as** (feminine).

os livros *the books*   **as casas** *the houses*

The forms of the definite article combine with the prepositions **de** and **em** as follows.

de + o:	do	de + os:	dos
de + a:	da	de + as:	das
em + o:	no	em + os:	nos
em + a:	na	em + as:	nas

VOCABULARY

agora now
ainda still, yet
aqui here
a ave the bird
o cão the dog
com with
em in, into, on, at
Filadélfia Philadelphia
o homem the man
a irmã the sister
o irmão the brother
o jardim the garden
o lente the professor
a lição the lesson
Lisboa Lisbon
mas but

morar to live
moro I live
mora (he or she) lives
moramos we live
moram (they) live
Nova York New York
onde? where?
o pàdeiro the baker
o pão the bread, loaf of bread; os pães
   the loaves of bread
quem? who?
o Rio (de Janeiro) Rio de Janeiro
o som the sound
o violino the violin
vizinho -a neighboring, next door

EXERCISES

A. *Translate the English words to complete the phrase or sentence.*
1. O cão *of the* homens.   2. Uma casa *with a* jardim.   3. *In the* casa de João.   4. As lições *of the* irmãos.   5. As *sisters* do homem.
6. Os *men* com os *loaves of bread.*   7. Onde *does* João *live?*   8. *He lives* no Rio.   9. *We live* na casa vizinha.

B. *Translate.*   1. Os cães do lente.   2. No jardim da casa.   3. As lições da irmã.   4. O som dos violinos.   5. Os pães do pàdeiro.
6. Os irmãos dos homens.   7. Os sons das aves.   8. As irmãs de João.   9. Casas com jardins.   10. As janelas do hotel.

C. *Translate.*   1. Onde mora o irmão de João?   2. Mora em Filadélfia.   3. A irmã mora ainda no Rio de Janeiro?   4. Sim, ainda mora no Rio.   5. Moramos em Lisboa agora mas os irmãos moram em Nova York.   6. Moro aqui e o lente mora na casa vizinha.   7. Quem mora na casa?   8. Moro na casa mas João mora no hotel.   9. Onde mora o homem?   10. Mora na casa com jardim.

D. *Translate.* 1. The sound of the violin. 2. The bread of the bakers. 3. The men with the dogs. 4. The bakers with the loaves of bread. 5. Who lives in the hotel? 6. The professor lives in the hotel. 7. Where do the men live? 8. They live in the house next door. 9. We live in Philadelphia, but the professor lives in Lisbon. 10. They live in Rio de Janeiro.

Lesson III

56. Formation of plural. Nouns ending in a consonant sound.

1. Nouns ending in **r, s,** or **z** form their plural by adding **-es.**

flọr	*flower*	flọres	*flowers*
mês	*month*	mẹses	*months*
vọz	*voice*	vọzes	*voices*

a) The following nouns ending in -s remain unchanged in the plural.

lápis	*pencil*	lápis	*pencils*
pịres	*saucer*	pịres	*saucers*

2. Nouns ending in -l form their plural by dropping the l and adding -is.

animạl	*animal*	animạis	*animals*
papẹl	*paper*	papéis	*papers*

57. Present indicative of the three conjugations.

There are three conjugations in Portuguese, and they are indicated by the ending of the infinitive: **-ar** (first conjugation), **-er** (second conjugation), and **-ir** (third conjugation).

	falạr	*to speak*	aprendẹr	*to learn*	partịr	*to leave*
	SINGULAR		**SINGULAR**		**SINGULAR**	
1.	fạl-o	*I speak*	aprẹnd-o		pạrt-o	
2.	(fạl-as)	*thou speakest*	(aprẹnd-es)		(pạrt-es)	
3.	fạl-a	*he, she, it speaks*	aprẹnd-e		pạrt-e	
	PLURAL		**PLURAL**		**PLURAL**	
1.	fal-ạmos	*we speak*	aprend-ẹmos		part-ịmos	
2.	(fal-ạis)	*you speak*	(aprend-eis)		(part-ịs)	
3.	fạl-am	*they speak*	aprẹnd-em		pạrt-em	

The second person forms of verbs and pronouns are placed in parentheses in this book. They are not used in conversational Portuguese. See section 58.

58. Second person.

The second person forms of the verb are not used in conversational Portuguese (except that the second singular is used in very familiar speech in Portugal, not in Brazil).   Instead of them, the third person forms are used with various nouns to which the value of the second person pronoun is attributed.   The commonest of such nouns is **o senhor** (**a senhora, os senhores, as senhoras**), e.g., **O senhor fala inglês** *You speak English,* **Os senhores falam inglês** *You* (pl.) *speak English.*   Other expressions with this value are **Vossa Excelência** [1] (**Vossas Excelências**), used in Portugal in polite conversation among equals or to a superior, **você** (**vocês**), used among friends or to a subordinate, and **a senhorita,** used in Brazil in addressing a young unmarried lady.[2]   These nouns are not repeated as frequently as *you* is in English.

VOCABULARY

alemão German
aprender to learn
espanhol Spanish
estudar to study
a **flor** the flower
francês French
o **jornal** the newspaper
o **lápis** the pencil
mal badly, poorly
o **mês** the month
muito very; much, hard
o **papel** the paper
o **pires** the saucer

pouco little
que? what?
o **senhor** the gentleman, sir, Mr.; you
a **senhora** the lady, young lady, Mrs.; you
a **senhorita** (*Brazilian*) the young lady, Miss, you
trabalhar to work
você you
Vossa Excelência Your Excellency, you
a **voz** the voice

EXERCISES

A. *Translate the English words to complete the phrase or sentence.*
1. As *voices* dos senhores.   2. As senhoras com os *newspapers.*   3. *The flowers* do lente.   4. Que *are you studying?*   5. *I am studying* português.   6. *We are learning* a falar português.   7. *They work* muito.   8. Aprendemos *German* e *French.*

[1] The abbreviation of **Vossa Excelência** is **V.Exª.**
[2] In Portugal, **a senhora** is generally used in addressing a young unmarried lady.

B. *Translate.* 1. As flores da senhora. 2. Os meses das flores. 3. O som das vozes. 4. Os jornais do lente. 5. O lápis do senhor. 6. A voz de João. 7. Os lápis da irmã. 8. Os pires da senhora.

C. *Translate.* 1. Que estuda o senhor? 2. Estudo o alemão. 3. Aprende V.Exª. (*Brazilian:* o senhor) a falar espanhol? 4. Não, senhor, não aprendo a falar espanhol, aprendo a falar francês. 5. Trabalha você muito? 6. Não trabalho muito, trabalho pouco. 7. Fala V.Exª. (*Brazilian:* o senhor) bem o português? 8. Não, senhor, falo o português muito mal. 9. Os senhores estudam muito? 10. Sim, senhor, estudamos muito.

D. *Translate.* 1. The voices in the garden. 2. The man with the papers (documents). 3. The flowers in the windows. 4. The newspapers of the lady. 5. Are you learning to speak French? 6. Yes, sir, I am learning to speak French and also Spanish. 7. Do you (pl.) study much? 8. No, sir, we do not study much. 9. Do you work hard? 10. Yes, sir, I work hard.

Lesson IV

59. Formation of feminine of adjectives. 1. Adjectives ending in -o form their feminine by changing -o to -a.

MASC.		FEM.
frio	*cold*	fria
branco	*white*	branca

2. Adjectives ending in -ão form their feminine by changing **-ão** to **-ã.**

MASC.		FEM.
alemão	*German*	alemã
são	*healthy*	sã

3. Adjectives ending in -e remain unchanged in the feminine.

MASC.		FEM.
doce	*sweet*	doce
pobre	*poor*	pobre

4. Adjectives ending in -m remain unchanged in the feminine.

	MASC.		FEM.
	comum	*common*	comum
	jovem	*young*	jovem
Exception:	bom	*good*	boa

5. Adjectives ending in a consonant generally remain unchanged in the feminine.

MASC.		FEM.
cortês	*polite*	cortês
azul	*blue*	azul
simples	*simple*	simples

Except adjectives of nationality:

MASC.		FEM.
inglês	*English*	inglêsa
espanhol	*Spanish*	espanhola

6. The feminine of **mau** *bad* is **má.** The adjective **só** *only, alone* is the same in both genders.

24

60. Formation of plural of adjectives. The plural of adjectives is formed like the plural of nouns.

1. Adjectives ending in a vowel (oral or nasal) or a nasal diphthong form their plural by adding -s.

SINGULAR		PLURAL
frio	*cold*	frios
fria	*cold*	frias
doce	*sweet*	doces
são	*healthy*	sãos
sã	*healthy*	sãs
alemão	*German*	alemães (exception)
alemã	*German*	alemãs

2. Adjectives ending in -m form their plural by changing this **m** to n and adding -s.

jovem	*young*	jovens
comum	*common*	comuns
bom	*good*	bons

3. Adjectives ending in -r, -s, or -z form their plural by adding -es.

	elementar	*elementary*	elementares
	cortês	*polite*	corteses
	feliz	*happy*	felizes
Exception:	simples	*simple*	simples

4. Adjectives ending in -l form their plural by dropping this l and adding -is.

azul	*blue*	azuis
possível	*possible*	possíveis
espanhol	*Spanish*	espanhóis

a) If the vowel preceding the l is accented i, this i and the i of -is contract to a single i.

civil	*civil*	civis

b) If the vowel preceding the l is unaccented i, this i becomes e before the addition of -is.

fácil	*easy*	fáceis
útil	*useful*	úteis

61. Agreement and position of adjectives. Adjectives agree in gender and number with the noun they modify. They generally follow the noun they modify.

homem são	*healthy man*
homens sãos	*healthy men*
pessoa sã	*healthy person*
pessoas sãs	*healthy persons*

The adjectives **bom** and **mau** often precede the noun they modify.

um bom cavalo	*a good horse*
um mau escritor	*a poor writer*

62. Present indicative of *ser to be.*

sou	*I am*	somos	*we are*
(és)	*thou art*	(sois)	*you are*
é	*he, she, it is*	são	*they are*

VOCABULARY

aplicado -a studious
azul blue
bom, boa good, kind
em breve soon
cortês polite
desejar to wish, desire
difícil difficult, hard
doce sweet, gentle
elementar elementary
fácil easy
feliz happy
frio -a cold
já now, at once
jovem young

mau, má bad, unkind
a moça (*Brazilian*) the girl
para for, to, towards
partir to leave
a pessoa the person
pobre poor
porque because
porquê? why?
a rapariga the girl; *see* moça *above*
o rapaz the boy
são, sã healthy
ser to be
simples simple
útil useful

EXERCISES

A. *Read.* João estuda o português. As lições são difíceis mas João é muito aplicado. Deseja morar em Lisboa para aprender o português bem. Parte em breve para Lisboa. José deseja partir com João. São felizes porque partem para Lisboa.

B. *Answer in Portuguese.* **1.** Quem estuda o português? **2.** São difíceis as lições de João? **3.** João é aplicado? **4.** Onde deseja João morar? **5.** Porquê deseja morar em Lisboa? **6.** Quem deseja partir com João para Lisboa? **7.** Porquê são felizes João e José?

C. *Translate the English words to complete the sentence.* **1.** Os rapazes são *polite*. **2.** As janelas são *blue*. **3.** As lições são *simple* e *easy*. **4.** As irmãs são muito *healthy*. **5.** As lições são *difficult*. **6.** *We wish* aprender o espanhol. **7.** *You wish* morar no Rio.

D. *Translate.* **1.** João é muito são. **2.** Os homens franceses são corteses. **3.** As portas são azuis. **4.** As lições elementares são fáceis e simples. **5.** É um mês muito frio. **6.** Os livros são bons e úteis. **7.** São vozes muito doces. **8.** São pessoas muito jovens e felizes. **9.** Somos rapazes pobres. **10.** As raparigas (*Brazilian:* moças) são más (*fem. pl. of* **mau**) para os irmãos. **11.** São senhoras portuguesas. **12.** É uma senhora espanhola.

E. *Translate.* **1.** Que deseja V.Exª. (*Brazilian:* o senhor) estudar? **2.** Desejo estudar o português. **3.** João deseja partir? **4.** Sim, senhor, deseja partir já. **5.** Desejamos lições fáceis. **6.** Os rapazes desejam morar em Lisboa. **7.** Desejo aprender a falar português. **8.** Estudam muito e aprendem pouco. **9.** Os senhores desejam morar em Filadélfia? **10.** Não, senhor, não desejamos morar em Filadélfia, desejamos morar no Rio.

F. *Translate.* **1.** The boys are kind to the sister. **2.** The lesson is very simple. **3.** The voices of the girls are sweet. **4.** They are very poor boys. **5.** I wish to live in New York. **6.** Do you wish to study with John? **7.** No, sir, I do not wish to study with John. **8.** The gentlemen are very polite. **9.** I wish to leave for (**para**) Lisbon now. **10.** She is a very polite person. **11.** The girl is Portuguese. **12.** They are Spanish gentlemen. **13.** They are studious.

Lesson V

63. Present indicative of *estar* *to be*.

estou	*I am*	estamos	*we are*
(estás)	*thou art*	(estais)	*you are*
está	*he, she, it is*	estão	*they are*

64. Use of *ser* and *estar*.

These two verbs mean *to be*. The basic difference between them is that **ser** expresses a permanent or characteristic state of being while **estar** expresses a temporary or accidental state of being.

Spanish cannot always be safely followed as a guide to the use of **ser** and **estar** in Portuguese.

1. The basic difference between **ser** and **estar** is found in their use with predicate adjectives.

O amigo é cego.	*The friend is blind.*
O ferro é duro.	*Iron is hard.*
João está doente.	*John is ill.*
A casa está cheia.	*The house is full.*

a) In accordance with this principle an adjective may have one value with **ser** and another with **estar**.

O hotel é bom.	*The hotel is good.*
O aluno está bom.	*The pupil is well.*
O hábito é mau.	*The habit is bad.*
A criança está má.	*The child is naughty.*
O gêlo é frio.	*Ice is cold* (characteristically).
A água está fria.	*The water is cold* (accidentally).

Unlike Spanish **malo**, Portuguese **mau** with **estar** does not mean *ill*. Use **mal** or doente: A criança está mal or doente *The child is ill*.

b) **Ser** and **estar** are similarly used with past participles functioning as adjectives.

O telhado é coberto com telhas.	*The roof is covered with tiles.*
O telhado está coberto de neve.	*The roof is covered with snow.*

Note the difference between this and the Spanish usage.

28

For **ser** used to form the passive voice, see section 145.

c) Sometimes **estar** with predicate adjective or past participle expresses in accordance with this principle a state of being of recent origin.

O café é caro.	*Coffee is dear.*
O café está caro.	*Coffee is dear now (has just gone up).*
A porta é pintada de verde.	*The door is painted green.*
A porta está pintada de fresco.	*The door is freshly painted.*

d) **Ser** is used with **rico, pobre, jovem (novo)**, and **vélho** because these adjectives represent characteristic and relatively permanent states of being.

João é rico e Maria é pobre.	*John is rich and Mary is poor.*

2. The basic difference between **ser** and **estar** is generally observed in their use to express location or position.

Onde é a biblioteca?	*Where is the library?*
Onde está João?	*Where is John?*

Note the difference between this and the Spanish usage.

3. Special uses of **ser.**

a) **Ser** is always used when the predicate is a substantive (noun or pronoun).

Somos amigos.	*We are friends.*
É médico.	*He is a physician.*

b) **Ser** is generally used in impersonal expressions.

É verdade.	*It is true.*
É possível.	*It is possible.*

For other special uses of **ser,** see sections 74 and 145.

4. Special use of **estar.** **Estar** is used with **a** plus the infinitive or with the gerund (**-ando, -endo, -indo**) to express an action in progress. The construction with **a** plus the infinitive is preferred in Portugal but not used in Brazil. This construction is somewhat similar to the progressive form in English.

Está a dormir. ⎫	
Está dormindo. ⎭	*He is sleeping.*

VOCABULARY

o actọr the actor
o advogạdo the lawyer
a água the water
ausẹnte absent
ɔ americ̣ano the American
caminhạr to walk
em cạsa at home, home
para cạsa de to the home of
cansạdo -a tired
casạdo -a married
cẹgo -a blind
chẹio -a full
a cidạde the city
a clạsse the class
cobẹrto -a covered
comprịdo -a long
estạr to be
a estrạda the road
estrẹito -a narrow
ficạr to stay, remain
a gẹnte people; tôda a gẹnte everybody; see todo o mundo below
họje today
jụntos -as together

lọnge (de) far (from)
magoạdo -a sore
o médico the physician
mẹsmo -a same
o mụndo the world; tọdo o mụndo (Brazilian) everybody
o pé the foot
a pẹdra the stone
a pẹna the trouble; é pena it is a pity
pẹrto (de) near
pọbre poor
precịso -a necessary
preparạr to prepare
presẹnte present
quẹnte hot
rịco -a rich
a rụa the street
sẹmpre always
o soldạdo the soldier
soltẹiro -a single, unmarried
o teạtro the theater
é tẹmpo de it is time to
tọdos everybody
é verdạde it is true

EXERCISES

A. *Read.* Maria mora na cidade. Está hoje em casa. Está preparando a sua lição. A casa de Ana é longe da cidade. Ana deseja estudar com Maria. Caminha na estrada para a casa de Maria. A estrada é muito má, está coberta de pedras. Os pés de Ana estão magoados. Mas agora estão juntas a estudar.

B. *Answer in Portuguese.* 1. Onde está Maria hoje? 2. Que está preparando? 3. É perto a casa de Ana? 4. Com quem deseja Ana estudar? 5. Onde caminha Ana? 6. É boa a estrada? 7. Estão magoados os pés de Ana? 8. Estão juntas Maria e Ana?

C. *Translate the English words to complete the sentence.* 1. O teatro *is* perto. 2. *We are* cansados. 3. João *is* ausente da classe.

4. *I am* em casa.   **5.** Os pés de João *are* magoados.   **6.** O homem *is* muito pobre.   **7.** O irmão de João *is* cego.   **8.** *It is* fácil aprender inglês.   **9.** *It is* tempo de partir.   **10.** *I am* advogado.   **11.** *We are* casados.

D. *Translate.*   **1.** A cidade está cheia de soldados.   **2.** A rua é muito estreita.   **3.** O rapaz está ausente da classe.   **4.** Hoje estão todos presentes.   **5.** A água está muito quente.   **6.** Todos desejam ser felizes.   **7.** Deseja o senhor ficar em casa?   **8.** Sim, senhor, estou em casa e desejo ficar em casa.   **9.** Onde é o teatro?   **10.** O teatro é na mesma rua.   **11.** O actor está agora no teatro.   **12.** A estrada é coberta com pedras.   **13.** A rua Garrett é perto.   **14.** Maria está longe agora.   **15.** São casados.   **16.** A irmã de Maria é muito rica.   **17.** O irmão é solteiro.   **18.** A estrada é comprida.

E. *Translate.*   **1.** O senhor é actor.   **2.** São advogados.   **3.** Sou português.   **4.** É médico.   **5.** Somos americanos.   **6.** É tempo de partir.   **7.** É preciso estudar muito.   **8.** Não é fácil aprender o português.   **9.** Não é verdade.   **10.** É pena.   **11.** João está a trabalhar (*Brazilian:* trabalhando).   **12.** Estamos a estudar (*Brazilian:* estudando) o espanhol.   **13.** A casa é longe do teatro.   **14.** Aqui estou longe de V.Exª. (*Brazilian:* do senhor).   **15.** Tôda a gente (*Brazilian:* todo o mundo) está a estudar (*Brazilian:* estudando) o português.   **16.** Os soldados estão cansados.

F. *Translate.*   **1.** The theater is full.   **2.** Everybody is absent today.   **3.** The road is narrow.   **4.** The air is always cold here.   **5.** We are at home.   **6.** I am an American.   **7.** It is necessary to leave now.   **8.** They are studying.   **9.** They are very poor.   **10.** We wish to stay home.   **11.** It is time to study.   **12.** It is true.   **13.** We are far from Lisbon now.   **14.** The house is near the road.   **15.** We are married.   **16.** They are tired.   **17.** John is poor.   **18.** They are unmarried.

Lesson VI

65. Present indicative of *fazer to make, do.*

faço	fazęmos
(fazes)	(fazęis)
faz	fązem

66. Demonstrative adjectives and pronouns.

MASC.		FEM.
êste	*this, this one*	ęsta
êstes	*these*	ęstas
êsse	*that, that one* (near you)	ęssa
êsses	*those*	ęssas
aquêle	*that, that one* (yonder)	aquęla
aquêles	*those*	aquęlas

Êste corresponds to the first person in that it refers to something (or someone) near the speaker; **êsse** corresponds to the second person in that it refers to something (or someone) near the person spoken to; and **aquêle** corresponds to the third person in that it refers to something (or someone) near the person or thing spoken of.

The accented **e** is close in all the masculine forms, while it is open in all the feminine forms.

These words are used as adjectives and as pronouns. When used as adjectives they agree in gender and number with the noun they modify. When used as pronouns they agree in gender and number with the noun they stand for.

êste livro	*this book*	**êste**	*this one* (i.e., book)
estas mesas	*these tables*	**estas**	*these* (i.e., tables)

67. Neuter demonstrative pronouns.

įsto	*this*
įsso	*that* (near person spoken to)
aquįlo	*that* (near person or thing spoken of)

32

These forms are used only as pronouns.   They do not stand for nouns but in an indeterminate way for previous statements or propositions.

Isso é certo.   *That is true.*

68. Demonstrative adjectives and pronouns (continued). The forms listed in sections 66 and 67 combine with the prepositions **de** and **em** as follows.

dêste	dęsta	disto
dêstes	dęstas	
dêsse	dęssa	disso
dêsses	dęssas	
daquêle	daquęla	daquilo
daquêles	daquęlas	
nêste	nęsta	nisto
nêstes	nęstas	
nêsse	nęssa	nisso
nêsses	nęssas	
naquêle	naquęla	naquilo
naquêles	naquęlas	

69. Indefinite article (continued). The forms of the indefinite article combine with the preposition **em** as follows.

em + um: num   em + uma: numa

70. Cardinal numerals from 1 to 20.

1	um, uma	9	nove	16	dezassęis
2	dois, duas	10	dęz		dezessęis (*Brazilian*)
3	três	11	onze	17	dezassęte
4	quatro	12	doze		dezessęte (*Brazilian*)
5	cinco	13	tręze	18	dezóito
6	sęis	14	catorze	19	dezanove
7	sęte		quatorze (*Brazilian*)		dezenove (*Brazilian*)
8	oito	15	quinze	20	vinte

These numerals are invariable except **um** and **dois,** which have feminine forms.

VOCABULARY

a to
aí there (*near the person spoken to*)
ali there (*near the person or thing spoken of*)
o aluno the pupil, the student
àmanhã tomorrow
o ano the year
contar to count; to intend, expect
o dia the day
a estação the season
fazer to make, do
Que tempo faz? How is the weather?
Faz bom tempo. It (*the weather*) is fine.
Faz mau tempo. It (*the weather*) is bad.
Faz frio. It is cold.
Faz calor. It is hot.
Faz vento. It is windy.
fora outside
geralmente generally

grande large, big
há there is, there are
importante important
o inverno the winter
já already
a mesa the table
o outono the autumn
outro -a other, another
passar to spend
pequeno -a little, small
um pouco a little
a primavera the spring
o professor the professor
quadrado -a square
quantos -as? how many?
que? o que? what?
redondo -a round
a semana the week
o tempo the weather
vélho -a old
o verão the summer

EXERCISES

A. *Read.* Há dez alunos na classe. Trabalham muito. Estudam o português. Um dos alunos conta de um a dez e outro já fala um pouco. Desejam passar o verão em Lisboa para aprender bem o português. Não faz calor naquela cidade no verão; geralmente faz bom tempo. O professor mora ali êste verão.

B. *Answer in Portuguese.* 1. Quantos alunos há na classe? 2. Trabalham muito? 3. O que fazem? 4. Contam em português? 5. Falam português? 6. Porquê desejam passar o verão em Lisboa? 7. Que tempo faz em Lisboa no verão? 8. Onde mora o professor êste verão?

C. *Translate the English words to complete the sentence.* 1. Estudo *these* lições. 2. Moramos *in this* casa. 3. A mesa *of that* rapaz é quadrada. 4. *That* é o livro de João. 5. *I intend* passar o

verão em Lisboa.   6. João mora *in that* hotel.   7. *It is* muito frio.
8. *There are* dez lições no livro.

D. *Translate.*   1. Que faz o senhor?   2. Estudo esta lição de
português.   3. O que fazem os senhores?   4. Trabalhamos nesta
cidade.   5. O que fazem aquêles rapazes com aquêle livro vélho?
6. Estudam a lição de português para àmanhã.   7. Que tempo faz
hoje?   8. Faz mau tempo e faz vento.   9. Porquê fica o senhor em
casa?   10. Fico em casa porque faz muito frio fora.   11. Que
tempo faz no verão?   12. Geralmente faz muito calor.

E. *Translate.*   1. Esta mesa é quadrada mas essa é redonda.
2. Esta casa é muito grande mas aquela é pequena.   3. Isso é importante.   4. Moro aqui nesta casa.   5. O senhor mora aí nessa casa.
6. João mora ali naquela casa.   7. Quantos dias há numa semana?
8. Há sete dias numa semana.   9. Quantas estações há no ano?
10. Há quatro estações no ano; são a primavera, o verão, o outono, e
o inverno.   11. Conto de um a dez: um, dois, três, quatro, cinco,
seis, sete, oito, nove, dez.   12. Contamos passar a primavera naquela cidade vélha.   13. O amigo conta passar o verão no Rio.
14. As janelas desta casa são grandes.

F. *Translate.*   1. What is John doing?   2. He is studying Portuguese.   3. How is the weather?   4. The weather is fine.   5. What
do you do in the winter?   6. I generally spend the winter in Lisbon.
7. How many lessons are there in this book?   8. There are twenty
lessons in that book.   9. There are twelve windows in that house.
10. I expect to spend the autumn in that hotel.   11. That is not
very important.   12. These men are still young, but those are very
old.   13. This book is large, but that one is small.   14. The brother
of that gentleman is old.

Lesson VII

71. Present indicative of *ir* *to go*.

vou	vamos
(vais)	(ides)
vai	vão

72. Special uses of *ir* and *acabar de*.

The verb **ir,** followed by an infinitive, may be used to express future action or state. The English equivalent is the progressive form of *to go*.

Vou estudar a minha lição.   *I am going to study my lesson.*

The present tense of **acabar de,** followed by an infinitive, may be used to express action in the recent past.[1] The English equivalent is *to have just*.

Acabo de estudar a minha lição.   *I have just studied my lesson.*

73. Possessive adjectives and pronouns.

MASC.		FEM.
o meu	*my, mine*	a minha
os meus		as minhas
(o teu)	*thy, thine*	(a tua)
(os teus)		(as tuas)
o seu	*his, her(s), your(s)*	a sua
os seus		as suas
o nosso	*our(s)*	a nossa
os nossos		as nossas
(o vosso)	*your(s)*	(a vossa)
(os vossos)		(as vossas)
o seu	*their(s), your(s)*	a sua
os seus		as suas

These forms are used as adjectives and as pronouns. They agree in gender and number with the thing possessed, not with the possessor. Thus, in **o meu lápis e a minha pena** *my pencil and pen,*

---

[1] The preterit of **acabar de** may be used with the same time reference, e.g., **Acabei de estudar a minha lição** *I have just studied my lesson.*

36

the possessor is the same person but **meu** is masculine because the thing possessed is masculine and **minha** is feminine because the thing possessed is feminine.   Accordingly, **seu** may mean *his* or *her* and **sua** may mean *his* or *her*, **seu** being used when the thing possessed is masculine and **sua** when the thing possessed is feminine.

o seu lápis	*his* or *her pencil*
a sua pena	*his* or *her pen*

a) Just as the third person forms of the verb are used for the second person forms (see section 58), so the third person forms of the possessive adjective and pronoun are used for the second person forms.   Therefore, the forms of **seu** may mean *your* (adjective) and *yours* (pronoun).

b) These words are often used without the definite article:

1. In direct address:

   Venha cá, meu amigo!   *Come here, my friend!*

2. With names of relatives in the singular:

   Meu pai está em casa.   *My father is home.*

3. In the predicate after forms of **ser,** except for emphatic distinction of possessors:

	O livro é meu.	*The book is mine.*
But	**O livro é o meu, não é o seu.**	*The book is mine, it is not his.*

c) Possessive adjectives are used much less in Portuguese than in English whenever possession is clear without them, particularly with parts of the body and articles of clothing.

O que tem na mão?	*What do you have in your hand?*
Vou tirar o chapéu.	*I am going to take my hat off.*

74. Special use of *ser*.   The verb **ser** followed by **de** is used to express possession and origin.

Êste lápis é de João.	*This pencil is John's.*
Sou do Brasil.	*I am from Brazil.*

75. Definite article (continued).   The forms of the definite article combine with the preposition **a** as follows.

$$a + o: \quad ao \qquad\qquad a + os: \quad aos$$
$$a + a: \quad à \qquad\qquad a + as: \quad às$$

76. Movement to or towards.   Movement to or towards a place is generally indicated by the preposition **para.**   But after **ir** *to go* and **vir** *to come*, both **a** and **para** are used, **a** for brief stay, **para** for more definite and continued destination.

Parto àmanhã para Lisboa.	*I leave tomorrow for Lisbon.*
Vou ao teatro esta tarde.	*I am going to the theater this afternoon.*
João vai para casa.	*John is going home.*

VOCABULARY

acabar to end, terminate, finish
alugar to rent
o amigo the friend
a bibliotęca the library
o Brasil Brazil
o chapéu the hat
donde? from where?
os Estados Unidos the United States
ir to go
ir para casa to go home
ir às compras to go shopping; *see*
   ir fazer compras *below*
(ir) fazer compras (*Brazilian*) to go
   shopping

a mãe the mother
a medicina the medicine
   para onde? where? (i.e., whither?)
a pęna the pen
Portugal [1]
procurar to look for, seek
o quarto the room
   de quęm? whose?
o sapato the shoe
   tirar to take off
o trabalho the work
   vago unoccupied, not taken

EXERCISES

A. *Read.*   O meu amigo é de Portugal.   Deseja ir às compras (*Brazilian:* ir fazer compras) àmanhã.   Vai comprar sapatos e um chapéu e deseja alugar um quarto.   Não vai morar na nossa casa porque não há quartos vagos.   Acaba de falar com seu irmão e agora conta passar o inverno em Nova York a estudar (*Brazilian:* estudando) medicina.

B. *Answer in Portuguese.*   1. Donde é o seu amigo?   2. O que deseja fazer àmanhã?   3. O que vai comprar?   4. E o que deseja

[1] Most names of countries are used with the definite article.   The word **Portugal** is an exception.

alugar? 5. Porquê não aluga um quarto na nossa casa? 6. Com quem acaba de falar? 7. Onde conta passar o inverno? 8. O que conta fazer em Nova York?

C. *Translate the English words to complete the sentence.* 1. Para onde *are you going*? 2. *I am going* às compras (*Brazilian:* fazer compras). 3. *They are going* alugar uma casa. 4. *I have just* aprender a lição. 5. Estudo *my* lições. 6. *Your* amigo trabalha muito. 7. Fica *in his* hotel. 8. Êstes chapéus são *ours.* 9. Moro *in your* casa. 10. *We are* do Brasil. 11. Vou *home.*

D. *Translate.* 1. O senhor vai estudar a sua lição? 2. Sim, senhor, vou estudar a minha lição. 3. Os meus amigos vão passar o verão em Lisboa. 4. De quem são êstes livros? 5. Êstes livros são nossos. 6. De quem é esta pena? 7. Esta pena é minha. 8. O meu amigo e o seu vão para Nova York. 9. Para onde vai sua mãe? 10. Minha mãe vai às compras (*Brazilian:* faz compras). 11. Acabam de partir. 12. Acabamos o nosso trabalho. 13. João mora na minha casa. 14. Vai ficar no seu hotel.

E. *Translate.* 1. João estuda a sua lição. 2. Maria estuda a sua lição. 3. Vou para Nova York àmanhã. 4. O que procura o senhor? 5. Procuro um hotel nesta rua. 6. Desejo alugar uma casa nesta cidade. 7. Maria está em casa. 8. João vai para casa. 9. Acaba de tirar o chapéu. 10. Procuro o irmão. 11. Vou tirar os sapatos. 12. Esta pena é minha e aquela é sua. 13. Esta pena é a minha, não é a sua. 14. Donde é o senhor? 15. Sou dos Estados Unidos. 16. João é de Portugal.

F. *Translate.* 1. He has just taken his hat off. 2. She is looking for her hat. 3. My friends finish their work. 4. They are going shopping in this street. 5. We intend to rent a house in this city. 6. Whose book is this? 7. It is your book. 8. Where are you going? 9. I am going to the library. 10. We are going to study our lessons tomorrow. 11. Where are you (pl.) from? 12. We are from the United States. 13. Whose houses are these? 14. They are ours.

Lesson VIII

77. Present indicative of *dar* *to give.*

dọu	dạmos
(dás)	(dạis)
dá	dão

78. Personal pronouns. Forms used as subject.

ęu	I	nós	*we*
(tụ)	*thou*	(vós)	*you*
êle	*he, it*	êles	*they* m.
ęla	*she, it*	ęlas	*they* f.

These pronouns are used for emphasis, contrast, and clarity (i.e., to avoid ambiguity).

Eu estudo muito.	*I study hard.*
Êle vai para Nova York mas ela fica aqui.	*He is going to New York, but she is staying here.*

a) The second person forms are not used in conversational Portuguese. They are replaced by various nouns having the value of pronouns. See section 58.

79. Telling time.

Que horas são?	*What time is it?*
É uma (hora).	*It is one o'clock.*
São duas (horas).	*It is two o'clock.*
São três (horas) e dez (minutos).	*It is ten minutes past three o'clock.*
São três (horas) menos dez (minutos).	*It is ten minutes to three.*
São quatro (horas) e um quarto.	*It is a quarter past four.*
São cinco (horas) e meia.	*It is half past five.*
É meio-dia.	*It is twelve o'clock noon.*
É meia-noite.	*It is twelve o'clock midnight.*
São dez em ponto.	*It is exactly ten o'clock.*
Vai nas onze.	*It is going on eleven o'clock.*
A que horas . . . ?	*At what time . . . ?*
À uma (hora).	*At one o'clock.*
Às duas (horas).	*At two o'clock.*
Ao meio-dia.	*At noon (at twelve o'clock noon).*
À meia-noite.	*At midnight (at twelve o'clock midnight).*

The words in parentheses may be omitted without changing the meaning.

In railroad schedules and in radio, theater, and motion-picture announcements, the cardinal numerals from 13 to 24 are used to designate the hours from 1 P.M. to 12 midnight.

Às quinze e meia.   *At half past three (in the afternoon).*

80. Names of the days of the week.

domingo	*Sunday*	quarta-feira	*Wednesday*
segunda-feira	*Monday*	quinta-feira	*Thursday*
têrça-feira	*Tuesday*	sexta-feira	*Friday*
	sábado	*Saturday*	

The word **feira** is often omitted. **Sábado** and **domingo** are masculine, and the rest of these words are feminine.

81. *Que?* **and** *qual?* *what?* Standing in questions before forms of the verb *to be, what* is translated by **que** (or **o que**) if a definition is asked for, otherwise by **qual** (pl. **quais**). Standing before a noun, *what* is translated by **que.**

Que é a capital dum país?   *What is the capital of a country?*
Qual é a capital de Portugal?   *What is the capital of Portugal?*
Que capital é perto de aqui?   *What capital is near here?*

VOCABULARY

até until
a **avenida** the avenue
cada each, every
o **cinema** the motion picture
o **comboio** the train; *see* **trem** *below*
começar to begin
como as
dar to give; to strike
dar com to encounter, run into
dar para to overlook, face
dar um passeio to take a walk
depois (*adv.*) afterwards; **depois de** (*prep.*) after

dias úteis workdays
o **dinheiro** the money
então then
a **escola** the school
a **hora** the hour; time, o'clock
a **língua** the language
menos less
o **número** the number
o **parque** the park
quando when
seguinte following
terminar to end
o **trem** (*Brazilian*) the train

EXERCISES

A. *Read.* Hoje é segunda-feira. João acaba de dar com sua irmã na avenida. Êle deseja ir ao teatro mas ela deseja ir ao cinema. Como faz calor, dão um passeio no parque. Então vão ao cinema. E depois vão para casa preparar as suas lições para o dia seguinte. Já são onze e estudam até à meia-noite.

B. *Answer in Portuguese.* 1. Com quem acaba de dar João na avenida? 2. O que deseja fazer João? 3. O que deseja fazer a irmã? 4. Que tempo faz? 5. Onde dão um passeio? 6. Para onde vão então? 7. Para onde vão depois do cinema? 8. O que fazem em casa? 9. A que horas começam a estudar? 10. Que horas são quando terminam as suas lições?

C. *Translate the English words to complete the sentence.* 1. *He* dá um passeio mas *I* fico em casa. 2. Estas janelas *face* a avenida. 3. *What* é o nome do seu amigo? 4. *What* combóio (*Brazilian:* trem) parte às oito? 5. Em *what* avenida mora seu irmão? 6. *It is* três menos cinco. 7. Nós *are taking* um passeio na avenida. 8. Não há classe de português nas *Tuesdays* e *Thursdays*. 9. O combóio (*Brazilian:* trem) de Lisboa parte *at half past one*.

D. *Translate.* 1. Vou dar o meu livro ao rapaz. 2. Elas dão os seus livros à escola. 3. Dou dinheiro aos meus amigos. 4. Nós damos pão aos soldados. 5. Esta janela dá para o jardim. 6. As janelas desta casa dão para a avenida. 7. Acabamos de dar com o nosso amigo na rua. 8. Eu dou um passeio no jardim cada dia da semana. 9. Ela dá um passeio na avenida. 10. Dão quatro horas. 11. Quando parte você para a escola? 12. Parto às sete e meia para a escola.

E. *Translate.* 1. Que horas são? 2. São duas horas e cinco. 3. A que horas parte o combóio (*Brazilian:* trem)? 4. O combóio (*Brazilian:* trem) parte às dezasseis (*Brazilian:* dezesseis) menos dez minutos. 5. O cinema começa às vinte e meia. 6. A escola termina às duas e um quarto. 7. Há cinema nas segundas, quartas, e sextas. 8. Não vou trabalhar no sábado. 9. Que dia da semana é hoje? 10. É domingo.

F. *Translate.* 1. Quais são os nomes dos dias da semana? 2. São domingo, segunda-feira, têrça-feira, quarta-feira, quinta-feira, sexta-feira, e sábado. 3. Qual é o número de alunos na classe? 4. O número de alunos é catorze. 5. Que língua fala êle? 6. Fala a língua portuguesa. 7. Qual é a língua do Brasil? 8. É a língua portuguesa. 9. Em que rua mora o seu amigo? 10. O meu amigo mora na rua Garrett. 11. Quais são os dias úteis? 12. Os dias úteis são a segunda, a têrça, a quarta, a quinta, a sexta, e o sábado.

G. *Translate.* 1. He gives his money to his friends. 2. That window faces the street. 3. I just ran into John. 4. We are taking a walk in the garden. 5. It is striking five. 6. What time is it? 7. It is a quarter to nine. 8. School begins at eight o'clock. 9. There is no school on (**aos**) Saturday. 10. Today is Friday. 11. In what street do you live? 12. I live in Garrett Street. 13. He is going to study his lesson on (**no**) Sunday. 14. Tuesday [1] and Wednesday [1] are workdays. 15. When does the train leave? 16. It leaves at a quarter past eleven.

[1] Use the definite article.

Lesson IX

82. Present indicative of *dizer* to say, tell **and** *ter* to have, possess.

digo	tenho
(dizes)	(tens)
diz	tem
dizemos	temos
(dizeis)	(tendes)
dizem	têm and teem

83. Preterit indicative. 1. Of regular verbs. In the preterit indicative of regular verbs, the accent falls on the endings and the dominant vowel of the endings is the same as the vowel of the ending of the infinitive.

falar	aprender	partir
SINGULAR	SINGULAR	SINGULAR
1. fal-ei	aprend-i	part-i
2. (fal-aste)	(aprend-este)	(part-iste)
3. fal-ou	aprend-eu	part-iu
PLURAL	PLURAL	PLURAL
1. fal-ámos	aprend-emos	part-imos
2. (fal-astes)	(aprend-estes)	(part-istes)
3. fal-aram	aprend-eram	part-iram

2. Of irregular verbs. Most irregular verbs have preterits which are irregular (1) because they are accented on the root (instead of the ending) in the first and third singular forms, (2) because the dominant vowel of the ending is ę, and (3) because they have a stem which is different from the stem of the infinitive.

dizer	fazer	estar	ter
SINGULAR	SINGULAR	SINGULAR	SINGULAR
1. disse	fiz	estive	tive
2. (dissęste)	(fizęste)	(estivęste)	(tivęste)
3. disse	fêz	estęve	tęve

44

	PLURAL	PLURAL	PLURAL	PLURAL
1.	dissẹmos	fizẹmos	estivẹmos	tivẹmos
2.	(dissẹstes)	(fizẹstes)	(estivẹstes)	(tivẹstes)
3.	dissẹram	fizẹram	estivẹram	tivẹram

a) The preterits of **dar, ir,** and **ser** are otherwise irregular. And those of **ir** and **ser** are identical.

	dar	ir	ser
	SINGULAR	SINGULAR	SINGULAR
1.	dẹi	fui	fui
2.	(dẹste)	(foste)	(foste)
3.	dẹu	foi	foi
	PLURAL	PLURAL	PLURAL
1.	dẹmos	fomos	fomos
2.	(dẹstes)	(fostes)	(fostes)
3.	dẹram	foram	foram

84. Use of preterit indicative. The preterit indicative is used to express simple action or state in the past, that is, action or state without reference to repetition or continuity. The time referred to is past from the point of view of the present, but it may be close to the present or remotely past. It is the tense of simple narration in the past.

> **Falei hoje com o seu amigo.**   *I spoke with your friend today.*
> **Aprendi o inglês na minha mocidade.**   *I learned English in my youth.*

This tense performs most of the functions of both the preterit and the perfect in Spanish.

85. Names of the months.

janeiro	*January*	julho	*July*
fevereiro	*February*	agôsto	*August*
março	*March*	setembro	*September*
abril	*April*	outubro	*October*
maio	*May*	novembro	*November*
junho	*June*	dezembro	*December*

The days of the month are designated by the cardinal numerals (section 70) except that the *first* is designated by the ordinal **pri-**

meiro.   And the definite article is not used with the cardinals except in the expression **o dia** + cardinal.

o primeiro de fevereiro (*Brazilian:* **dia**	
primeiro de fevereiro)	*the first of February*
cinco de julho	*the fifth of July*
o dia cinco de julho	*the fifth of July*

English *on* with these expressions is translated by the preposition **em.**

no primeiro (*Brazilian:* **em primeiro**)	
de fevereiro	*on the first of February*
em cinco de julho	*on the fifth of July*
no dia cinco de julho	*on the fifth of July*

VOCABULARY

apenas only
a casa de to the home of
dizer to say, tell
o ensejo (de) the opportunity (to)
  estar com fome to be hungry
  estar com sêde to be thirsty
  estar com vontade de to have a notion to, wish to, be anxious to
examinar to examine
fazer a chamada to call the roll
as férias grandes (*Brazilian:* as grandes férias) the summer holiday *or* vacation
há ago
a manhã the morning
a mão the hand
muito -a much, many
muito tempo a long time
a noite the night, the evening
ontem yesterday
ontem à noite last night, last evening
passado -a last

pensar (em) to think (of)
não . . . senão only, nothing but
a tarde the afternoon, the evening
ter to have, possess
ter (muita) fome to be (very) hungry
ter sêde to be thirsty
ter (muito) frio to be (very) cold
ter calor to be warm, be hot
ter sono to be sleepy
ter saudades de to long for, to be homesick for, to miss
ter vontade de to have a notion to, wish to, be anxious to
ter que + *infinitive* to have to
ter + *noun* + para to have . . . to
ter tempo para to have the time to
ter . . . anos to be . . . years old
Quantos anos tem . . .?   How old is . . .?
trinta thirty
a verdade the truth

EXERCISES

A. *Read.*   A escola terminou a semana passada em cinco de junho.   Ontem à noite fomos a casa do professor.   Êle falou do seu trabalho e tivemos o ensejo de examinar os seus livros. Tem uma grande biblioteca. Esta manhã João disse—Isso é muito interessante mas eu agora não penso senão nas férias grandes (*Brazilian:* grandes férias). Já começaram a semana passada.

B. *Answer in Portuguese.* 1. Quando terminou a escola? 2. Para onde foram ontem à noite? 3. De que falou o professor? 4. O que examinaram? 5. Tem o professor muitos livros? 6. São interessantes os livros do professor? 7. Pensam em livros? 8. Em que pensam agora? 9. Quando começaram as férias grandes (*Brazilian:* grandes férias)?

C. *Translate the English words to complete the sentence.* 1. Partimos *on the tenth* de agôsto. 2. *We told* a verdade. 3. O professor *called the roll* às dez. 4. *We went* a Nova York a semana passada. 5. *He had* muito trabalho *to* fazer. 6. *I ran into* seu irmão na avenida hoje. 7. *We worked* naquela cidade o ano passado. 8. *It is* frio aqui no inverno. 9. *I am* muito frio mas João *is* calor. 10. *They learned* a falar português em Lisboa. 11. *They have to* estudar a sua lição. 12. João *misses* os seus irmãos.

D. *Translate.* 1. Êle diz a verdade aos amigos. 2. Eu digo a verdade a tôda a gente (*Brazilian:* todo o mundo). 3. O senhor diz sempre isso. 4. O que tem o senhor na mão? 5. Tenho os meus livros na mão. 6. Tenho vontade de ir a Nova York. 7. Quantos anos tem o seu irmão? 8. Tem dezanove (*Brazilian:* dezenove) anos. 9. Temos muitas lições para estudar. 10. Estou com vontade de dar um passeio. 11. Êle tem sêde. 12. Nós estamos com muita fome. 13. Êles têm muito trabalho para fazer. 14. Tenho muito calor. 15. Não tenho tempo para ir ao teatro esta noite. 16. Tenho saudades dos meus amigos no Rio.

E. *Translate.* 1. Onde esteve o senhor a semana passada? 2. Estive em Lisboa a semana passada. 3. João foi ao Rio o ano passado. 4. Estudou êle a sua lição esta manhã? 5. Sim, senhor, estudou (he did). 6. Tive o ensejo de ir ao teatro ontem à noite. 7. Morámos em Filadélfia há muito tempo. 8. Trabalharam nesta casa hoje. 9. O lente fêz a chamada às oito e meia. 10. Dei um passeio no jardim esta manhã. 11. Dei com o nosso amigo na rua esta tarde. 12. O combóio (*Brazilian:* trem) partiu às nove da manhã. 13. Aprenderam o português há dois anos. 14. Ontem foi quinta-feira.

F. *Translate.* 1. Quantos meses há no ano? 2. Há doze meses no ano. 3. Quais são os meses da primavera? 4. Os meses da primavera são março, abril, e maio. 5. Quantos dias há no mês de setembro? 6. Há trinta dias no mês de setembro. 7. Que dia do mês é hoje? 8. Hoje é dois de outubro. 9. E ontem, que dia do mês foi? 10. Ontem foi o primeiro (*Brazilian:* Ontem foi dia primeiro). 11. Há apenas vinte e oito dias no mês de fevereiro.

G. *Translate.* 1. They had a notion to take a walk last night. 2. Did you study your lesson today? 3. Yes, sir, I studied (it). 4. They had to go to school today. 5. We are always hungry. 6. How old is your brother? 7. My brother is twenty years old. 8. I was still sleepy this morning. 9. What day of the month is today? 10. Today is the ninth. 11. I call the roll every morning at a quarter past nine. 12. There are only ten pupils in the class. 13. We went to New York yesterday. 14. What are the months of winter? 15. The months of winter are December, January, and February. 16. We are homesick for our house in New York.

Lesson X

86. Present and preterit indicative of *poder* *to be able, can* and *ver* *to see.*

PRESENT

posso	vejo
(podes)	(vês)
pode	vê
podemos	vemos
(podeis)	(vêdes)
podem	vêem

PRETERIT

pude	vi
(pudeste)	(viste)
pôde	viu
pudemos	vimos
(pudestes)	(vistes)
puderam	viram

87. Commands. The command form is made by dropping the ending **-o** of the first singular present indicative and adding

  -e (sg.) or **-em** (pl.) if the verb is an **-ar** verb;
  -a (sg.) or **-am** (pl.) if the verb is an **-er** or an **-ir** verb.

falar	fal-o	fal-e	fal-em	*speak*
aprender	aprend-o	aprend-a	aprend-am	*learn*
partir	part-o	part-a	part-am	*leave*
fazer	faç-o	faç-a	faç-am	*do*

The subject, **o senhor, Vossa Excelência,** etc., is often expressed and placed after the verb.

Fale o senhor mais de-vagar.   *Speak more slowly.*

a) The command forms of four of the irregular verbs which we have had cannot be derived in this way.

dar	dou	dê	dêem	*give*
estar	estou	esteja	estejam	*be*
ser	sou	seja	sejam	*be*
ir	vou	vá	vão	*go*

49

88. Cardinal numerals (continued from section 70).

21	vinte-e-um (uma)	101	cento-e-um (uma)
22	vinte-e-dois (duas)	102	cento-e-dois (duas)
23	vinte-e-três	103	cento-e-três
24	vinte-e-quatro	199	cento-e-noventa-e-nove
25	vinte-e-cinco	200	duzentos, -as
26	vinte-e-seis	201	duzentos-e-um (uma)
27	vinte-e-sete	300	trezentos, -as
28	vinte-e-oito	400	quatrocentos, -as
29	vinte-e-nove	500	quinhentos, -as
30	trinta	600	seiscentos, -as
31	trinta-e-um (uma)	700	setecentos, -as
32	trinta-e-dois (duas)	800	oitocentos, -as
40	quarenta	900	novecentos, -as
41	quarenta-e-um (uma)	1,000	mil
50	cinqüenta	1,001	mil-e-um (uma)
60	sessenta	2,000	dois mil
70	setenta	3,000	três mil
80	oitenta	100,000	cem mil
90	noventa	1,000,000	um milhão
100	cem	2,000,000	dois milhões

Note that *a hundred* and *a thousand* are expressed by **cem** and **mil** respectively without the indefinite article.

The word for *100* is **cem** but *hundred* from *101* to *199* inclusive is expressed by **cento**.

In compound numbers from *21* to *999* inclusive, **e** *and* is placed between all the single numbers forming the compound.

In numbers beginning with *1,000*, **mil** is preferable to the full *hundreds*.

       mil novecentos-e-quarenta-e-dois   *1942*

89. Ordinal numerals.

first	primeiro -a		*sixth*	sexto -a
second	segundo -a		*seventh*	sétimo -a
third	terceiro -a		*eighth*	oitavo -a
fourth	quarto -a		*ninth*	nono -a
fifth	quinto -a		*tenth*	décimo -a

In the names of kings, popes, etc., the ordinals are used up to
décimo *tenth* only. Above **décimo** the cardinals are used.

Manuel Segundo	*Manuel II*
Leão Treze	*Leo XIII*

VOCABULARY

atęnto -a attentive
a bondạde (de) the kindness (to)
comprạr to buy
de-pressa fast, quickly
de-vagạr slow, slowly
escutạr to listen to
gloriọso glorious
a gravạta the necktie
o imperadọr the emperor
a livrarịa the bookstore
a lọja the store
Luịz Louis
a lụva the glove

mạis more
o nasciminto the birth
ęsta nọite this evening, tonight
ọnde where, in which
ọntem à tạrde yesterday afternoon
podęr to be able, can
o rẹi the king
tão so
tọdo, tôda all, whole, every
último -a last
vendęr to sell
vẹr to see

EXERCISES

A. *Read.* **1.** Maria não pôde ir ao teatro ontem à tarde porque
teve que trabalhar.   Trabalha numa livraria, uma loja onde vendem
livros.   Há dez mil livros na livraria.   E venderam mil-e-quinhen-
tos livros no mês passado.   Vi Maria esta manhã.   Está cansada.
Não vai trabalhar esta tarde.   Vai ao cinema.

B. *Answer in Portuguese.* **1.** Porquê não pôde ir Maria ao
teatro ontem à tarde?   **2.** Onde trabalha Maria?   **3.** O que é uma
livraria?   **4.** Quantos livros há na livraria onde Maria trabalha?
5. Quantos livros venderam no mês passado?   **6.** Quando viu você
Maria?   **7.** Maria está cansada?   **8.** O que vai fazer esta tarde?

C. *Translate the English words to complete the sentence.* **1.** *Have*
a bondade de dar estas luvas à sua irmã.   **2.** *Listen to* o professor.
3. *Be* bom para tôda a gente (*Brazilian:* todo o mundo).   **4.** Há
thirty alunos nesta classe.   **5.** *Go* à loja procurar os sapatos.
6. João não *could* ver o nome da rua.   **7.** *They saw* o meu amigo

ontem à noite. 8. *Give* (pl.) os seus livros ao professor. 9. *You saw* o cinema esta tarde. 10. *Don't speak* tão de-pressa. 11. *Do* o seu trabalho esta manhã. 12. *Learn* a sua lição hoje.

D. *Translate.* 1. O senhor pode ir ao teatro esta noite? 2. Não, senhor, não posso. 3. Não pudemos ver o seu amigo. 4. Vi o irmão de Maria esta manhã. 5. Vemos o irmão de João tôdas as manhãs. 6. Onde podemos comprar luvas? 7. Podem comprar luvas naquela loja. 8. João viu o meu livro nesta mesa. 9. Onde viram os senhores o meu amigo? 10. Vimos o seu amigo na rua Garrett. 11. Pôde o senhor ver o número da casa? 12. Não pude ver aquêle número.

E. *Translate.* 1. Escutem os alunos. 2. Estudem e trabalhem muito. 3. Estejam atentos às palavras do professor. 4. Dê um passeio tôdas as manhãs. 5. Faça a chamada às nove. 6. Fale de-vagar. 7. Não fale tão de-pressa. 8. Tenha a bondade de falar mais de-vagar. 9. Vá à biblioteca procurar os livros. 10. Aprendam os alunos bem as suas lições. 11. Diga sempre a verdade. 12. Dêem os livros aos alunos.

F. *Translate.* 1. Pode contar de um a cem? 2. Sim, senhor, posso. 3. Quantos livros tem o senhor na sua biblioteca? 4. Tenho cento-e-oitenta-e-sete livros na minha biblioteca. 5. Quantos dias tem um ano? 6. Um ano tem trezentos-e-sessenta-e-cinco dias. 7. Quantos alunos há nesta classe? 8. Há trinta-e-seis alunos nesta classe. 9. Que lição estudamos hoje? 10. Estudamos a décima lição. 11. Manuel Primeiro foi um bom rei. 12. Luiz Catorze (*Brazilian:* Quatorze) foi um rei glorioso.

G. *Translate.* 1. I can go to the theater this afternoon. 2. Did you see my brother at the theater? 3. Yes, I saw your brother at the theater. 4. I see your sister every morning. 5. You can buy gloves and neckties in this store. 6. Speak faster. 7. Call the roll more slowly. 8. Look for my books on the table. 9. The month of January has thirty-one days. 10. The year of his birth was 1894. 11. There are five hundred books in her library. 12. Pedro II was Emperor of (**do**) Brazil.

Lesson XI

90. Present indicative and preterit indicative of *saber to know, know how, learn, find out about* and *vir to come.*

PRESENT

sei	venho
(sabes)	(vens)
sabe	vem
sabemos	vimos
(sabeis)	(vindes)
sabem	vêm and veem

PRETERIT

soube	vim
(soubeste)	(vieste)
soube	veio
soubemos	viemos
(soubestes)	(viestes)
souberam	vieram

91. Personal pronouns. Forms used as object of verb.

me	*me, to or for me*	nos	*us, to or for us*
(te)	*thee, to or for thee*	(vos)	*you, to or for you*
o	*him, it, you*	os	*them, you*
a	*her, it, you*	as	*them, you*
lhe	*to or for him, her, it, you*	lhes	*to or for them, you*

These pronouns are used only as direct or indirect objects of a verb.

In the first and second persons (sg. and pl.) the same form is used as direct and indirect object while in the third person (sg. and pl.) there are different forms for direct and indirect object. (In Brazilian Portuguese **lhe** and **lhes** are used as direct and indirect objects.)

The third person forms may refer to **Vossa Excelência, o senhor,** etc., and may, therefore, mean *you* or *to you* (sg. and pl.). See section 58.

Vejo-o.	*I see you.*
Digo-lhe a verdade.	*I tell you the truth.*

92. Personal pronouns.   Position of forms used as object of verb.
The pronouns listed in section 91 above sometimes precede and sometimes follow the verb.   When they follow the verb, they are attached
to it with a hyphen.
1. They follow the verb in independent positive sentences (declarative, interrogative, and imperative, i.e., in commands) except
as noted in 2 c, d, and e below.

Vi-o esta manhã.	*I saw him this morning.*
Deram-lhe o livro?	*Did they give him the book?*
Diga-me a verdade.	*Tell me the truth.*

2. They precede the verb
   a) in independent negative sentences (declarative, interrogative, and imperative, i.e., in commands):

Não o vi esta manhã.	*I did not see him this morning.*
Não lhe deram o livro?	*Did they not give him the book?*
Não me diga a verdade.	*Don't tell me the truth.*

   b) in dependent clauses of all kinds: [1]

Sei que me diz a verdade.	*I know that he tells me the truth.*
Êste é o lugar onde o vi.	*This is the place where I saw him*

   c) in independent interrogative sentences introduced by interrogative pronouns and adverbs:

Quem lhe disse isso?	*Who told you that?*
Onde os viu?	*Where did you see them?*

   d) in independent declarative sentences after certain common
   adverbs such as **ainda, assim, bem, já, logo, pouco, sempre,
   talvez,** and **também** and after the indefinite pronouns
   ambos, outros, todos, tudo, isto, and **isso.**

Sempre me diz a verdade.	*He always tells me the truth.*
Todos me dizem a mesma coisa.	*Everybody tells me the same thing.*

[1] In dependent negative clauses the pronoun may sometimes even precede
the word **não**: Sei que me não diz a verdade *I know that he does not tell me the
truth.*

e) in Brazilian Portuguese in independent positive sentences (declarative and interrogative) if the subject pronoun is expressed.

Eu o vi esta manhã.	*I saw him this morning.*
Êles lhe deram o livro?	*Did they give him the book?*

3. They sometimes precede and sometimes follow the infinitive:

Vim para o ver.	*I came in order to see him.*
Desejo dizer-lhe a verdade.	*I wish to tell you the truth.*

These pronouns are often omitted.

Viu o meu amigo hoje?	**Sim, vi.**	*Did you see my friend today?*
		Yes, I saw him.

VOCABULARY

brẹve shortly, presently
cẹdo early
fazẹr ụma pregụnta (*Brazilian:* per-gụnta) to ask a question
a **história** the history, the story
a **igrẹja** the church
a **mentịra** the lie
não . . . nạda nothing, not anything
a **notícia** the news

por by, for, after
preguntạr (*Brazilian:* **perguntạr**) to ask; **preguntạr por** to ask for
que who; (*conj.*) that
respondẹr to answer
sabẹr to know, know how, learn
tạrde (*adv.*) late
vịr to come
voltạr to return

EXERCISES

A. *Read.* Um homem veio à minha porta a semana passada. Disse-me o seu nome e preguntou (*Brazilian:* perguntou) por meu irmão. Respondi-lhe—Meu irmão não está em casa mas volta breve. Então o homem disse—Diga a seu irmão o meu nome e diga-lhe também que desejo falar-lhe.

B. *Answer in Portuguese.* 1. Quem veio à sua porta a semana passada? 2. Sabe o seu nome? 3. Por quem preguntou? 4. O que lhe respondeu? 5. Que disse o homem então?

C. *Translate the English words to complete the sentence.* 1. *I came* ver o seu irmão. 2. Acabo de *learn the news.* 3. *They learned* a notícia esta manhã. 4. *They came* de Portugal. 5. *I know* o seu nome. 6. *He told me* a verdade. 7. *They gave us* o dinheiro. 8. *I gave him* as suas luvas. 9. Eu *did not see her* ontem no teatro. 10. *He* sempre *gives me* dinheiro. 11. *I know* que *he gave you* o livro. 12. Desejou *to see me.*

D. *Translate.* 1. Sabe o senhor onde mora aquela senhora? 2. Não sei onde mora. 3. Os amigos veem aqui todos os dias. 4. Veio o senhor cedo? 5. Não, senhor, vim muito tarde. 6. Sei que o senhor veio tarde. 7. Donde vem o seu amigo? 8. Vem do Brasil. 9. Os alunos vieram comprar livros ontem. 10. São alunos que desejam vir estudar em Nova York. 11. Os senhores sabem as lições? 12. Não, senhor, não sabemos. 13. Quando soube a notícia? 14. Soube a notícia ontem à noite.

E. *Translate.* 1. Disse-lhe donde veio? 2. Não, senhor, não me disse donde veio. 3. Viram os senhores meu irmão esta manhã? 4. Não, senhor, não o vimos. 5. Sabe o senhor a verdade? 6. Sim, senhor, sei-a e digo-a sempre. 7. Fala o senhor inglês? 8. Sim, senhor, falo-o bem. 9. O que lhe disse aquêle senhor? 10. Não me disse nada. 11. Deu-lhes muito dinheiro? 12. Não nos deu nada. 13. Venha [1] ver-me esta tarde. 14. Tenho uma pregunta para fazer-lhe. 15. Eu dei-lhe (*Brazilian:* Eu lhe dei) muito dinheiro. 16. O senhor deu-nos (*Brazilian:* nos deu) o livro.

F. *Translate.* 1. I know where the house is. 2. Did you learn the news early? 3. Yes, I found out about it at six o'clock. 4. We came here to study Portuguese. 5. I told him the truth. 6. He always tells lies to me. 7. All the students know their lessons today. 8. We told them nothing. 9. I gave you all my books. 10. We come to this church every Sunday. 11. When did he tell you that story? 12. He told me that story yesterday. 13. He asks many questions.

[1] Command form of **vir.**

Lesson XII

93. Present and preterit indicative of *pôr* to *put*, *place* and *ler* to *read*.

PRESENT

ponho	leio
(põzes)	(lês)
põe	lê
pomos	lêmos
(pondes)	(lêdes)
põem and põe	lêem

PRETERIT

pus	li
(pusęste)	(lêste)
pôs	leu
pusęmos	lêmos
(pusęstes)	(lêstes)
pusęram	leram

The e of põ<es and põe is pronounced like English *y*.

94. Personal pronouns. Forms used as object of verb combined with each other.[1]

If two of the pronouns (one direct object and the other indirect object) listed in section 91 in the preceding lesson are used with the same verb, the indirect object pronoun always precedes the direct, and they combine as follows.

me + o:	mo	*it to me*	(te + o:	to)	*it to thee*
me + a:	ma	*it to me*	(te + a:	ta)	*it to thee*
me + os:	mos	*them to me*	(te + os:	tos)	*them to thee*
me + as:	mas	*them to me*	(te + as:	tas)	*them to thee*
lhe + o:	lho	*it to him, to her, to you, to them,* or *to you* (pl.)
lhe + a:	lha	*it to him, to her, to you, to them,* or *to you* (pl.)
lhe + os:	lhos	*them to him, to her, to you, to them,* or *to you* (pl.)
lhe + as:	lhas	*them to him, to her, to you, to them,* or *to you* (pl.)
nos + o:	no-lo	*it to us*	(vos + o:	vo-lo)	*it to you*
nos + a:	no-la	*it to us*	(vos + a:	vo-la)	*it to you*
nos + os:	no-los	*them to us*	(vos + os:	vo-los)	*them to you*
nos + as:	no-las	*them to us*	(vos + as:	vo-las)	*them to you*

[1] See section 98, 1 a.

Não mos deu.	*He did not give them to me.*
Disse-lho.	*I told him (you, them) so.*
Quem no-lo disse?	*Who told us so?*

a) Note that the **lh-** of **lho, lha, lhos,** and **lhas** has the value of **lhe** *to him, to her, to you* and of **lhes** *to them, to you* (pl.).

95. Personal pronouns. Forms used as object of verb combined with verb. 1. The third person forms **o, a, os,** and **as** listed in section 91 in the preceding lesson change to **-lo, -la, -los,** and **-las** respectively when attached to verb forms ending in **r** (all infinitives), **s** (most second singulars, all first plurals, most second plurals, and a few first and third singular preterits), and **z** (a few first and third singular preterits and a few third singular present indicatives) and the **r, s,** and **z** of the verb forms drop.

falar + o:	falá-lo	aprender + o:	aprendê-lo
(falas + o	fala-lo)	(aprendes + o:	aprende-lo)
falamos + o:	falamo-lo	aprendemos + o:	aprendemo-lo
(falais + o:	falai-lo)	(aprendeis + o:	aprendei-lo)
unir + o:	uni-lo	faz + o:	fá-lo
(unes + o:	une-lo)	fiz + o:	fí-lo
unimos + o:	unimo-lo		
(unis + o:	uni-lo)		

a) Note that in these combinations the acute accent is used to distinguish the infinitive of the first conjugation from the second singular and the circumflex accent to distinguish the infinitive of the second conjugation from the second singular.

2. The third person forms **o, a, os,** and **as** listed in section 91 in the preceding lesson change to **-no, -na, -nos,** and **-nas** respectively when attached to verb forms ending in a nasal vowel (all third plurals and a few third singulars).

dão + o:	dão-no	*they give it*
falam + o:	falam-no	*they speak it*
aprendem + o:	aprendem-no	*they learn it*

VOCABULARY

o **artigo** the article
barato cheap, cheaply
o **bilhete** the ticket
a **camisa** the shirt
caro -a dear
de-fronte across the street
a **estante** the bookcase
a **gaveta** the drawer

imediatamente at once, immediately, right away
lá there (*more remote than* **ali**)
ler to read
ou or
pois well
pôr to put, place
o **prato** the plate
sôbre on

EXERCISES

A. *Read.* O homem que veio à minha porta a semana passada voltou hoje. Meu irmão perguntou-lhe—Porquê deseja falar-me? O homem respondeu-lhe—Tenho uma casa para vender e desejo vender-lha. Meu irmão disse-lhe então—O senhor vê aquela casa de-fronte? Pois, acabamos de comprá-la ontem; venderam-no-la muito barato.

B. *Answer in Portuguese.* 1. Voltou o homem que veio à sua porta a semana passada? 2. Que tem o homem para vender? 3. Deseja vendê-la a seu irmão? 4. Porquê não lha (*it from him*) compra seu irmão? 5. A casa que comprou seu irmão foi cara?

C. *Translate the English words to complete the sentence.* 1. *They place* os livros na estante. 2. *They read* muitos livros. 3. *Read* êste jornal. 4. *Put* o prato sôbre a mesa. 5. *They placed* os jornais sôbre a mesa. 6. *I read* o seu artigo no jornal. *Translate the English words to complete the sentence and make any changes necessary in the ending of the verb.* 7. João deu *it to us.* 8. Lêmos *it* esta manhã. 9. Dei *it to him.* 10. Lêem *it* tôdas as manhãs. 11. Pusemos *them* sôbre a mesa. 12. Demos *it to them.* 13. Falam *it* bem. 14. Deu *me it.* 15. Aprendemos *it* de-pressa. 16. Deram *them to us.*

D. *Translate.* 1. Leu o jornal desta manhã? 2. Sim, senhor, li. 3. Leio todos os livros que o senhor me dá. 4. Ponho o prato sôbre a mesa. 5. Pôs o senhor os livros na estante? 6. Sim, senhor, pus. 7. Lêmos muitos livros todos os anos. 8. Pusemos os livros sôbre a mesa. 9. Êles põem as camisas na gaveta. 10. Os senhores lêem todos os jornais. 11. Leia [1] êste livro. 12. Ponha [2] essas camisas na gaveta.

E. *Translate.* 1. Deu o livro a João? 2. Sim, dei-lho. 3. Deu os lápis aos alunos? 4. Sim, dei-lhos. 5. Diz-me a verdade? 6. Sim, digo-lha. 7. Pôs os livros na estante? 8. Sim, senhor, pu-los lá. 9. Elas dão o dinheiro a João ou a Maria? 10. Dão-no a Maria. 11. Êles deram-lhes os bilhetes? 12. Sim, senhor, deram-no-los. 13. Lêem o jornal todos os dias? 14. Sim, senhor, lêmo-lo todos os dias. 15. Nós lêmos o português e aquêles rapazes lêem-no também. 16. Pomos os livros sôbre a mesa e êles põem-nos na estante.

F. *Translate.* 1. Did you put the books in the bookcase? 2. Yes, I put them there this morning. 3. Did you give the books to your pupils? 4. Yes, I gave them to them. 5. Did he give you the money? 6. Yes, he gave it to me right away. 7. Did they put the shirts in the drawer? 8. Yes, they put them there this morning. 9. Did they tell you the truth? 10. No, they did not. 11. Did he give us his newspapers? 12. Yes, he gave them to us. 13. Read this book, and put it in the bookcase. 14. Did you read those newspapers? 15. Yes, I read them yesterday.

[1] Command form of **ler.**
[2] Command form of **pôr.**

Lesson XIII

96. Personal pronouns. Forms used as object of a preposition.
1. The following pronouns are used as object of a preposition.

mim	*me*	nós	*us*
(ti)	*thee*	(vós)	*you*
êle	*him, it*	êles	*they* m.
ęla	*her, it*	ęlas	*they* f.

Comprou o livro para mim.	*He bought the book for me.*
A carta foi escrita por êles.	*The letter was written by them.*

2. The various nouns to which the value of second person pronouns is attributed (section 58) are also used with this same value as object of a preposition.

Comprei o bilhete para o senhor.	*I bought the ticket for you.*
A carta foi enviada por Vossa Excelência.	*The letter was sent by you.*

3. The reflexive pronoun **si** *himself, herself, itself, yourself, themselves, yourselves* is used as object of a preposition. It functions colloquially as a personal pronoun (nonreflexive) of the second person with a value approximately equivalent to **o senhor**.

Comprei o bilhete para si.	*I bought the ticket for you.*

This use is looked upon with much less favor in Brazil than in Portugal.

97. Personal pronouns. Forms used as object of a preposition (continued). 1. The third person forms listed in section 96 combine with the prepositions **de** and **em** as follows.

de + êle:	dêle	de + êles:	dêles
de + ęla:	dęla	de + ęlas:	dęlas
em + êle:	nêle	em + êles:	nêles
em + ęla:	nęla	em + ęlas:	nęlas

2. The following combinations take the place of the preposition **com** with the pronouns **mim, ti, nós, vós,** and **si**.

comigo	*with me*	connosco	*with us*
(contigo)	*with thee*	(convosco)	*with you*
consigo	*with himself, herself, itself, yourself, themselves,*		
	yourselves, and *with you* (sg. and pl.)		

a) Note that **consigo,** besides being reflexive, is used colloquially as a personal pronominal expression (nonreflexive) of the second person (see section 96, 3 above).

Vou consigo.   *I am going with you.*

98. Personal pronouns. Forms used as object of a preposition (continued). 1. The forms listed in section 96 above (including nouns with the value òf second person pronouns) are often used with the preposition **a** as indirect object of the verb instead of the indirect object pronouns listed in section 91. As they are strongly stressed, they are thus used for emphasis, and, as the third person forms are more definite in their reference, the latter are thus used also to avoid ambiguity.

Deu o livro a mim (for emphasis).   *He gave the book to me.*
Deu o livro a êle, a ela, ao senhor (to avoid ambiguity or for emphasis).   *He gave the book to him, to her, to you.*

a) In Brazilian Portuguese this construction is favored even when the direct object is a personal pronoun, in order to avoid the combinations **mo, lho, no-lo,** etc.

Não os deu a mim.   *He did not give them to me.*

2. The third person forms listed in section 96 above (and the nouns with the value of second person pronouns) are often used with the preposition **de** to avoid ambiguity instead of the possessive adjective **seu.**

o seu livro	*his book, her book, their book, your book*
o livro dêle	*his book*
o livro dela	*her book*
o livro dêles	*their book*
o livro do senhor	*your book*
o livro dos senhores	*your book*

3. The third person forms listed in section 96 above (and the nouns with the value of second person pronouns) are often used with the preposition **de** to avoid ambiguity instead of the possessive pronoun **seu**.

A minha casa e a dêle (for a sua).	*My house and his.*
Tenho o livro dêle, não o dela (for o seu).	*I have his book, not hers.*
Comprei o meu bilhete e o do senhor (for o seu).	*I bought my ticket and yours.*

a) These expressions are used without the definite article in the predicate after forms of **ser**, except for emphatic distinction of possessors (see section 73, b 3).

	O livro é dêle.	*The book is his.*
But	O livro é o dêle, não é o dela.	*The book is his, it is not hers.*

VOCABULARY

ach**a**r to find
aqu**i** t**e**m here you have (*i.e.*, here is, here are)
atrás de behind
b**e**lo -a beautiful
a c**a**rta the letter
a ch**a**ve the key
a c**o**isa the thing
a confi**a**nça the confidence, trust

diante de in front of
entre between
interess**a**nte interesting
mat**e**rno -a maternal, mother
obrig**a**do -a thanks, thank you; muito obrig**a**do many thanks
o rel**ó**gio the clock
sent**a**do -a seated
visit**a**r to visit; to look at

EXERCISES

A. *Read.* A casa que comprámos tem um jardim atrás dela. O homem visitou a casa e viu nela muitas coisas interessantes. Deu um passeio no jardim connosco e viu nêle muitas e belas flores. Êle disse a meu irmão—Deseja vender-me esta casa? E meu irmão vendeu-lha. Aquêle homem veio para vender-nos uma casa e nós vendemos-lhe uma.

B. *Answer in Portuguese.* 1. O que tem a casa que compraram atrás dela? 2. O que viu o homem na casa quando a visitou? 3. Deu um passeio com os senhores no jardim? 4. O que viu no jardim? 5. Que disse a seu irmão? 6. O que fêz seu irmão? 7. De quem é a casa agora?

C. *Translate the English words to complete the sentence.* 1. Está sentado atrás de *you.* 2. Êste livro é *his*, não é *yours.* 3. Dei os lápis *to them.* 4. Foram *with you.* 5. Comprei o chapéu para *her.* 6. É *their* casa e moram *in it.* 7. Aqui tem o jornal da manhã; há coisas muito interessantes *in it.* 8. O relógio está diante de *her.* 9. Veio *with me* ontem. 10. Tenho uma carta para *him.* 11. Fiz aquêle trabalho para *you.*

D. *Translate.* 1. João está sentado atrás de mim. 2. Comprei cinco livros para êle. 3. Fizeram muito trabalho para nós. 4. Está sentado entre êle e nós. 5. Vimos aqui com o senhor. 6. Comprei o jornal para o senhor. 7. Sabe o senhor o nome do homem que está sentado diante de si (*Brazilian:* do senhor)? 8. Não, senhor, não sei o nome do homem que está sentado diante de mim. 9. Tem muita confiança em mim. 10. Tenho uma carta para si (*Brazilian:* o senhor).

E. *Translate.* 1. O professor está sentado atrás da mesa e os alunos estão sentados diante dela. 2. É a minha casa e moro nela. 3. São bons livros e achamos muitas coisas interessantes nêles. 4. Vim aqui com o senhor. 5. Deseja o senhor ir comigo ao teatro? 6. Sim, senhor, desejo ir ao teatro consigo. 7. Disse-lhe o senhor a verdade? 8. Sim, disse-lha. 9. Deu-me o dinheiro? 10. Sim, dei-o ao senhor. 11. Deu o livro a João ou a Maria? 12. Dei-o a êle. 13. Diz-me a verdade mas não a diz a todos. 14. Deram a mim o dinheiro.

F. *Translate.* 1. Tenho os livros dêle. 2. De quem é êste chapéu? 3. É o chapéu do senhor. 4. João pôs o meu livro na minha gaveta e o livro dêle na gaveta dêle. 5. É a casa dêle ou a dela? 6. É a dela. 7. Aqui tem a sua chave. 8. Tenho a chave dêle. 9. O português é a sua língua materna. 10. Temos os bilhetes dêles. 11. Aqui têm os senhores os livros. 12. Muito obrigados. 13. Êsse dinheiro é dêle.

G. *Translate.* 1. We are seated behind him. 2. And they are seated in front of us. 3. We bought these books for you. 4. They have confidence in us. 5. They came here with us. 6. And I came here with you. 7. He gave me the books, and I gave him the money. 8. He gave them to me, and I gave it to him. 9. I found your money on the table. 10. They bought their books yesterday. 11. His keys are behind the clock. 12. Your letter came this morning. 13. These tickets are theirs. 14. This letter is his. 15. Here is your letter. 16. Many thanks.

Lesson XIV

99. Present indicative and preterit indicative of *querer to wish, want,*
will **and** *rir to laugh.*

PRESENT

quęro	rįo
(quęres)	(rįs)
quęr and quęre	rį
queręmos	rįmos
(queręis)	(rįdes)
quęrem	rįem

PRETERIT

quįs	rį
(quisęste)	(rįste)
quįs	rįu
quisęmos	rįmos
(quisęstes)	(rįstes)
quisęram	rįram

100. Imperfect indicative. 1. The imperfect indicative has only
two sets of endings, one for verbs of the first conjugation and one for
verbs of the second and third conjugations.

falar	aprender	partir
SINGULAR	SINGULAR	SINGULAR
1. fal-ava	aprend-įa	part-įa
2. (fal-avas)	(aprend-įas)	(part-įas)
3. fal-ava	aprend-įa	part-įa
PLURAL	PLURAL	PLURAL
1. fal-ávamos	aprend-íamos	part-íamos
2. (fal-áveis)	(aprend-íeis)	(part-íeis)
3. fal-avam	aprend-įam	part-įam

2. The imperfect indicatives of all regular and irregular verbs
are regular except those of **ser, ter, vir,** and **pôr.**

66

ser	ter	vir	pôr
SINGULAR	SINGULAR	SINGULAR	SINGULAR
1. ẹra	tịnha	vịnha	pụnha
2. (ẹras)	(tịnhas)	(vịnhas)	(pụnhas)
3. ẹra	tịnha	vịnha	pụnha
PLURAL	PLURAL	PLURAL	PLURAL
1. éramos	tínhamos	vínhamos	púnhamos
2. (éreis)	(tínheis)	(vínheis)	(púnheis)
3. ẹram	tịnham	vịnham	pụnham

a) Note that the imperfect indicatives of **ir** and **ver** are regular.

ir	ver
SINGULAR	SINGULAR
1. ịa	vịa
2. (ịas)	(vịas)
3. ịa	vịa
PLURAL	PLURAL
1. íamos	víamos
2. (íeis)	(víeis)
3. ịam	vịam

101. Use of imperfect indicative. The imperfect is used to express action or state in the past as continuing, repeated, or habitual. It can often be conveniently translated by the past progressive (*was* or *were* with the present participle), by *kept on* with the present participle, or by *used to* or *would* with the infinitive. This tense is the tense of description in the past.

Estudavam as suas lições.	*They were studying their lessons.*
Trabalhava a-pesar-da minha presença.	*He kept on working in spite of my presence.*
Iam à escola todas as manhãs às oito.	*They used to go to school every morning at eight o'clock.*
A casa tinha muitas janelas.	*The house had many windows.*

Two contrasted actions in the past may be expressed by two imperfect indicatives if both actions are simultaneous and continuing. If only one is continuing, it is expressed by the imperfect while the other is expressed by the preterit indicative.

Êle estudava enquanto eu trabalhava.   *He was studying while I was working.*
Êle estudava quando eu cheguei.   *He was studying when I arrived.*

For another important use of the imperfect indicative, see section 128.

VOCABULARY

abrir to open
ambos both
a casa de hóspedes the boardinghouse;
  see pensão *below*
contar to tell
enquanto while
entrar em to enter, go into, come into
o hóspede the guest

norte-americano -a American, North
  American
a palavra the word
ao passo que while
a pensão (*Brazilian*) boardinghouse
a pronúncia the pronunciation
querer to wish, want, will
querer dizer to mean
rir to laugh; rir de to laugh at

EXERCISES

A. *Read.* Tenho dois amigos norte-americanos que falam o português muito bem. Aprenderam-no em Coimbra e ambos têm uma boa pronúncia. Falam-no sempre quando estão juntos. Quando estavam em Coimbra, moravam numa casa de hóspedes (*Brazilian:* pensão) onde todos não falavam senão português. Agora contam ir ao Rio para lá estudar o português.

B. *Answer in Portuguese.* 1. Falam português os seus amigos norte-americanos? 2. Onde o aprenderam? 3. Falam muito o português? 4. Como o aprenderam? 5. O que contam fazer agora?

C. *Translate the English words to complete the sentence.* 1. *We were going* ao teatro. 2. *They used to come* aqui todos os dias. 3. Que *means* esta palavra? 4. *They laughed* de nós. 5. A mesa *was* redonda. 6. *We used to put* os livros na estante. 7. João *was finishing* o seu trabalho quando eu parti. 8. *I knew* a verdade enquanto êle *kept on telling* mentiras. 9. *They used to see us* na igreja. 10. *I had* muitos amigos no Rio.

D. *Translate.* 1. Quis dar um passeio no jardim. 2. Queremos comprar luvas nesta loja. 3. Êle riu muito de nós. 4. Rio das coisas que êles fazem. 5. O que quer dizer essa palavra? 6. Quer dizer "livro" em alemão. 7. De que ri o senhor? 8. Rio da história que me contou. 9. Os alunos querem os lápis? 10. Sim, querem-nos.

E. *Translate.* 1. Falava com o professor. 2. Aprendia a ler o espanhol. 3. Tínhamos muitos amigos em Lisboa. 4. Punham os livros na gaveta quando eu entrei. 5. Ria do homem que via na rua. 6. Vinha aqui todas as tardes. 7. Meu irmão não estava em casa. 8. Quando era jovem, morava em Paris. 9. Dizia-mo quando João entrou no quarto. 10. Nós trabalhávamos enquanto êles liam os jornais.

F. *Translate.* 1. I laughed at him. 2. He was laughing at me. 3. He used to live in the house next door. 4. He kept on opening the door for the guests. 5. We used to work in this city. 6. He wished to come to Philadelphia. 7. I was home when he told them the news. 8. What does this word mean? 9. I do not know what it means in Portuguese. 10. She studied her lesson while we took a walk. 11. I went home every night at ten o'clock. 12. What was your sister doing? 13. She was working in the garden. 14. We were not laughing at the professor. 15. What were you doing when the guests came into the room? 16. I was reading the newspaper.

Lesson XV

102. Present indicative and preterit indicative of *haver to have* **and** *trazer to bring*.

PRESENT

hei	trago
(hás)	(trazes)
há	traz
havemos	trazemos
(haveis)	(trazeis)
hão	trazem

PRETERIT

houve	trouxe [1]
(houveste)	(trouxeste)
houve	trouxe
houvemos	trouxemos
(houvestes)	(trouxestes)
houveram	trouxeram

103. Future indicative. There are two future indicatives: (1) a simple future, formed by attaching as endings to the infinitive the forms of the present indicative of **haver** (minus the initial **h** and the element **hav-** of the first and second plural forms), and (2) a compound future, formed by placing **de** plus the infinitive after the present indicative of **haver** with a hyphen between the forms of **haver** and **de**. The compound future expresses strong determination on the part of the subject.

falarei	hei-de falar
(falarás)	(hás-de falar)
falará	há-de falar
falaremos	havemos-de falar
(falareis)	(haveis-de falar)
falarão	hão-de falar

[1] The x of this tense and the derived tenses is pronounced like **ss** (section 45 b).

a) The future indicatives of all regular and irregular verbs are formed in these two ways except that the simple futures of the verbs **dizer, fazer,** and **trazer** are formed on shortened infinitives: **direi, farei,** and **trarei.**

104. Position of pronouns with simple future. 1. In independent affirmative sentences the pronouns listed in section 91 and their combinations with each other listed in section 94 are placed between the two elements of the simple future and connected with them by hyphens.

Falar-lhe-ei.	*I shall speak to him.*
Dir-me-á.	*He will tell me.*
Dir-lho-emos.	*We shall tell him (it).*
Dar-no-lo-á.	*He will give it to us.*

The forms **o, a, os,** and **as** change to **-lo, -la, -los,** and **-las** respectively because of the preceding infinitive, in accordance with section 95, 1. And accents are placed on **a** and **e** in accordance with section 95, 1 a.

Acabá-lo-ei.	*I shall finish it.*
Aprendê-lo-á.	*He will learn it.*
Fá-lo-emos.	*We shall do it.*
Di-lo-ão.	*They will tell it.*

2. In independent negative sentences, in independent interrogative sentences introduced by interrogative pronouns and adverbs, and in dependent clauses, all these pronouns and their combinations precede the simple future in accordance with section 92.

Não lhe falarei.	*I shall not speak to him.*
Quem mo dará?	*Who will give it to me?*
Diz que o fará.	*He says that he will do it.*

105. Other uses of *haver*. Besides being used to form the future indicative, **haver** is used impersonally with the meanings *there is, there are,* and *ago*. The impersonal forms of the tenses we have had are: present **há,** preterit **houve,** imperfect **havia,** future **há-de haver** and **haverá. Haver** never means *to have* in the sense of *to possess;* this meaning is expressed by **ter.**

VOCABULARY

o **acidente** the accident
acreditar to believe
alguma coisa something
àmanhã de manhã tomorrow morning
célebre famous
o **centro** the center
o **comércio** the business, commerce
o **copo** the glass, the tumbler
o **freguês** the customer
a **gente** the people
oito dias a week
o **pôrto** the harbor, the port
o **Pôrto** Oporto

poupar to save
próximo -a next
quinze dias two weeks
se if (*Brazilian:* si)
a **séde** the seat
na próxima semana next week
a semana que vem next week
sôbre about
trazer to bring
a **universidade** the university
a **viagem** the trip, the voyage
o **vinho** the wine
o **vinho do Pôrto** Port wine

EXERCISES

A. *Read.* Nós poupamos dinheiro para poder fazer uma viagem a Portugal. Iremos ali no próximo ano. Visitaremos Lisboa, o Pôrto, Coimbra, e outras cidades grandes e pequenas. Lisboa tem um grande e belo pôrto, o Pôrto é centro do comércio de vinhos que têm o nome de vinhos do Pôrto, e Coimbra é a séde duma célebre universidade. Falar-lhe-emos na próxima semana das outras cidades que vamos visitar.

B. *Answer in Portuguese.* 1. Porquê poupam dinheiro? 2. Quando irão a Portugal? 3. Que cidades visitarão? 4. O que há de interessante em Lisboa? no Pôrto? em Coimbra? 5. Diga-me alguma coisa sôbre as outras cidades que vão visitar.

C. *Translate the English words to complete the sentence.* 1. *I shall bring* os livros àmanhã. 2. *Did they bring* as luvas esta manhã? 3. *There were* muita gente na rua. 4. *You will know how* falar português em breve. 5. *They will have* mais lições *to* estudar. 6. Os fregueses *will not believe* a verdade. 7. Êle *will come* na próxima semana. 8. Sei que êle *will learn it.* 9. Êles *will come* àmanhã. 10. Estas lições são difíceis e nós *shall study them* muito. 11. Quantos alunos *were there* na classe? 12. Eu *shall bring you* um copo de água imediatamente.

D. *Translate.* 1. Há muita gente no teatro. 2. Havia vinte alunos naquela classe. 3. O amigo trouxe-me o jornal esta manhã às nove. 4. Trazia-mo às oito. 5. Traga [1]-me um copo de água. 6. Vi o professor há quinze dias. 7. Houve um acidente na rua. 9. O pàdeiro traz pão aos frègueses todos os dias. 10. Tra-lo todos os dias. 11. Veio aqui há oito dias.

E. *Translate.* 1. Iremos a Nova York na próxima semana. 2. Estarão juntos àmanhã. 3. Acredito que minha irmã virá àmanhã de manhã. 4. Dar-me-á os livros? 5. Sim, dar-lhos-ei. 6. Estudarão as lições? 7. Sim, senhor, estudá-las-emos. 8. Dir-nos-á a verdade? 9. Sim, dir-lha-ei. 10. Há de haver muita gente no teatro esta noite. 11. Acredito que o senhor há de aprender o português de-pressa. 12. Sim, aprendê-lo-ei de-pressa. 13. O senhor alugará a casa? 14. Sim, senhor, alugá-la-ei. 15. Trar-lhe-ei os seus livros àmanhã de manhã. 16. Aprenderão esta lição para àmanhã? 17. Sim, aprendê-la-emos. 18. Não, não a aprenderemos.

F. *Translate.* 1. I shall ask for him tomorrow morning. 2. We shall live in that hotel. 3. He will tell me where he was going. 4. Will they give you the books? 5. Yes, they will give them to me. 6. She will tell you. 7. Have you studied your lessons? 8. No, but we shall study them tomorrow morning. 9. Shall you be here next week? 10. Yes, I shall. 11. He will bring you a glass of water if you are thirsty. 12. There will be many students in that class. 13. I believe that he will do it. 14. We shall live together in Lisbon. 15. She was here two weeks ago. 16. We shall be customers in that store.

[1] Command form of **trazer.**

Lesson XVI

106. Present indicative and preterit indicative of *crer to believe, think* **and** *valer to be worth, be useful.*

PRESENT

creio	valho
(crês)	(vales)
crê	vale
cremos	valemos
(credes)	(valeis)
crêem	valem

PRETERIT

cri	vali
(crêste)	(valeste)
creu	valeu
cremos	valemos
(crêstes)	(valestes)
creram	valeram

Except in the present tense, **crer** is generally replaced by **acreditar.**

107. Reflexive pronouns and reflexive verbs. 1. Reflexive pronouns are direct and indirect object pronouns which refer to the same person or thing as the subject of the verb. They are the same as the personal pronouns listed in section 91 except in the third singular and plural.

me	*myself, to* or *for myself*	**nos**	*ourselves, to* or *for ourselves*
(te)	*thyself, to* or *for thyself*	**(vos)**	*yourselves, to* or *for yourselves*
se	*himself, to* or *for himself* *herself, to* or *for herself* *itself, to* or *for itself* *yourself, to* or *for yourself*	**se**	*themselves, to* or *for themselves* *yourselves, to* or *for yourselves*

2. Reflexive verbs are verbs used with reflexive pronouns to express an action of the subject upon itself. The reflexive pronouns

are placed with respect to the verb in accordance with section 92
(see section 104 for their position with respect to the simple future
indicative).   Thus the present indicative affirmative and negative
of **levantar-se** *to get up, rise* is conjugated as follows.   Note that the
final **s** of the first plural is dropped before **-nos** is added.

eu levanto-me *I get up*	eu não me levanto
(tu levantas-te)	(tu não te levantas)
êle levanta-se	êle não se levanta
ela levanta-se	ela não se levanta
o senhor levanta-se	o senhor não se levanta
nós levantamo-nos	nós não nos levantamos
(vós levantais-vos)	(vós não vos levantais)
êles levantam-se	êles não se levantam
elas levantam-se	elas não se levantam
os senhores levantam-se	os senhores não se levantam

a) The simple future indicative affirmative is **eu levantar-me-ei,**
etc.

b) Some verbs are not reflexive although their equivalents in
Spanish and other Romance languages are, e.g., **acordar** *to get awake*,
adormecer *to go to sleep*.   But in Brazilian Portuguese, *to get awake*
is preferably **acordar-se.**

108. Use of reflexive for the passive voice.   The reflexive is often
used where the passive voice would be used in English.

Falam-se muitas línguas naquela cidade.	*Many languages are spoken in that city.*
Dançava-se.	*Dancing was enjoyed* or *There was dancing.*

109. Impersonal use of reflexive.   The third singular reflexive is
often used impersonally.   This construction may be translated into
English by the verb with *one, they, you,* or *people* as subject.

Por onde se vai para a estação?	*Which way does one go to the station?*
Pode-se ver a tôrre da minha janela.	*The tower can be seen from my window.*

110. Reciprocal use of reflexive.   A plural subject may be looked
upon as acting upon itself as a whole although the individuals consti-

tuting it do not act upon themselves separately but rather upon each other. To express such action the reflexive construction is used in what is called the reciprocal use of the reflexive.

Vêem-se no espelho.	*They see each other in the mirror.*

In order to avoid ambiguity the indefinite pronoun construction **um ao outro** (**uma à outra**) is used where the subject consists of two individuals and **uns aos outros** (**umas às outras**) where the subject consists of more than two individuals.

Vêem-se no espelho um ao outro.	*They* (two individuals) *see each other in the mirror.*
Vêem-se no espelho uns aos outros.	*They* (more than two individuals) *see each other in the mirror.*
Escrevem-se cartas uns aos outros.	*They* (more than two individuals) *write letters to each other.*

a) Note that the preposition **a** is included in the indefinite pronoun construction whether the reflexive pronoun is direct or indirect.

VOCABULARY

acordar to get awake
adormecer to go to sleep
antes de before
o **assunto** the subject, the affair
a **cama** the bed
 certo -a sure
 chamar-se to be called; **chamo-me** my name is
 como? how?
a **conversa** the conversation
 conversar to converse
 crer to believe, think; **crer em** to believe in; **crer que sim** to think so; **crer que não** to think not
 deitar-se to lie down, go to bed
o **dia de anos** the birthday
a **estação** the station
 faltar a to be absent from

ir para a cama to go to bed
ir-se (embora) to go away
levantar-se to rise, get up
muitíssimo very much
muito . . . para too . . . to
nunca never
passar sem to do without
por ali that way
por aqui this way
por onde? which way?
por isso therefore
o **segrêdo** the secret
sem without
também não not either, neither
tanto (*adv.*) so much
ter razão to be right
valer to be worth
valer a pena to be worth while

EXERCISES

A. *Read.* Ontem à noite não me deitei antes da meia-noite. E não podia adormecer. Por isso, estou muito cansado para estudar esta manhã. Não sei a minha lição de português mas não quero faltar à classe hoje. Temos classe de conversa e passaremos o tempo conversando em português sôbre um assunto que nos deu o professor.

B. *Answer in Portuguese.* 1. A que horas deitou-se ontem à noite? 2. Adormeceu imediatamente? 3. Está cansado hoje? 4. Sabe a lição de português? 5. Como passarão o tempo na classe de português?

C. *Translate the English words to complete the sentence.* 1. João *got up* cedo esta manhã. 2. Maria *went to sleep* imediatamente. 3. Quando *will you get awake?* 4. Estou certo que êle *will not go to bed* antes da meia-noite. 5. *One can go* para a estação por ali. 6. Nós *see each other* cada segunda-feira. 7. Eu não tenho dinheiro e êle *either* não tem. 8. Êstes livros *are worth* muito. 9. Não posso *do without* os meus amigos. 10. Eu *shall not get up* antes das oito.

D. *Translate.* 1. Creio que há de vir àmanhã. 2. Acreditei que êle vinha mas ainda não veio. 3. Êstes livros valem muito. 4. Não vale a pena trabalhar tanto. 5. Cremos que valemos muito. 6. Crêem nas palavras do amigo. 7. Crê o senhor que virá esta noite? 8. Sim, estou certo que virá. 9. Esta casa valia muito mas agora não vale nada. 10. Creio que não vale a pena ir ali. 11. Crê que João o fará? 12. Creio que sim. 13. Creio que não. 14. Creio que tem razão.

E. *Translate.* 1. Levantámo-nos às sete. 2. Levanto-me cedo e deito-me tarde. 3. Não nos deitamos nunca antes das onze. 4. Como se chama aquêle rapaz? 5. Chama-se João. 6. Êle estudava quando nos fomos embora. 7. Deitar-se-ão às onze e meia. 8. Adormeci depois da meia-noite. 9. Acordei esta manhã muito cedo. 10. Estava cansado e deitei-me imediatamente.

F. *Translate.* 1. Fala-se português nesta loja. 2. Diz-se que êle tem muitos amigos. 3. Não se pode passar sem dinheiro. 4. Dizem-se muitos segredos uma à outra. 5. Damo-nos livros nos dias de anos. 6. Está certo que se verão no Rio. 7. Deitámo-nos depois de ler os jornais da tarde. 8. Vai-se a Coimbra por ali e a Lisboa por aqui. 9. Por onde se vai à estação? 10. Vai-se à estação por aqui. 11. É tarde e vou para a cama.

G. *Translate.* 1. These books are not worth anything. 2. Those pencils are not worth anything either. 3. I think they will come today. 4. Are you sure that he gets up early? 5. Yes, I know that he goes to bed early and gets up early. 6. They were tired and went to bed. 7. I went to sleep before ten o'clock. 8. They got awake very early. 9. We see each other every day. 10. We told each other many secrets. 11. Which way do you go to the library? 12. You go to the library that way. 13. I cannot do without books; I read very much. 14. Has John gone to sleep? 15. I think not; he is reading the morning paper. 16. They went away without their books. 17. That boy never gets up early.

Lesson XVII

111. Radical-changing verbs. Verbs with radical _e_. In addition to the change in ending, some verbs have a change in their radical vowel and are, therefore, called radical-changing verbs.

PRESENT INDICATIVE

1st Conjugation	2d Conjugation	3d Conjugation
SINGULAR	SINGULAR	SINGULAR
1. lẹvo	dẹvo	sịrvo
2. (lẹvas)	(dẹves)	(sẹrves)
3. lẹva	dẹve	sẹrve
PLURAL	PLURAL	PLURAL
1. levạmos	devẹmos	servịmos
2. (levạis)	(devẹis)	(servịs)
3. lẹvam	dẹvem	sẹrvem

The following observations apply to all tenses except the present subjunctive (see section 115 a).

In all forms in which radical **e** is not accented, it is pronounced like French mute _e_. In all forms in which radical **e** is accented, it is pronounced ẹ, with the exception of the first singular present indicative of verbs of the second conjugation, where it is pronounced ẹ, and the first singular present indicative of verbs of the third conjugation, where it is changed to ị. Thus the variations of radical **e** are the same in all three conjugations except in the first singular present indicative, where the first conjugation has ẹ, the second ẹ, and the third ị.

a) If radical **e** is followed by **m** + consonant or **n** + consonant, it is always pronounced ẹ nasalized whether accented or not accented, except in the first singular present indicative of verbs of the third conjugation, where it is changed to ị nasalized.

sẹnto	vẹndo	sịnto
(sẹntas)	(vẹndes)	(sẹntes)
sẹnta	vẹnde	sẹnte
sentạmos	vendẹmos	sentịmos
(sentạis)	(vendẹis)	(sentịs)
sẹntam	vẹndem	sẹntem

79

b) If radical **e** is followed by one of the palatal sounds—soft **g, j, ch, lh, nh, x,** or **s** (= *sh*)—it is pronounced like *i* in *perish* when unaccented, e.g., **aconselhar, mexer, vestir.**

112. Radical-changing verbs.   Verbs with radical *o.*

PRESENT INDICATIVE

1st Conjugation	*2d Conjugation*	*3d Conjugation*
SINGULAR	SINGULAR	SINGULAR
1. tǫmo	mǫvo	dụrmo
2. (tǫmas)	(mǫves)	(dǫrmes)
3. tǫma	mǫve	dǫrme
PLURAL	PLURAL	PLURAL
1. tomǎmos	movẹmos	dormĩmos
2. (tomǎis)	(movẹis)	(dormịs)
3. tǫmam	mǫvem	dǫrmem

The following observations apply to all tenses except the present subjunctive (see section 115 a).

In all forms in which radical **o** is not accented it is pronounced like *u* in *rule*. In all forms in which radical **o** is accented, it is pronounced **ǫ**, with the exception of the first singular present indicative of verbs of the second conjugation, where it is pronounced **ǫ**, and the first singular present indicative of verbs of the third conjugation, where it is changed to **ụ**. Thus the variations of radical **o** are the same in all three conjugations except in the first singular present indicative, where the first conjugation has **ǫ**, the second **ǫ**, and the third **ụ**.

a) If radical **o** is followed by **m** + consonant or **n** + consonant, it is always pronounced **ǫ** nasalized whether accented or not accented.

cǫnto	rǫmpo
(cǫntas)	(rǫmpes)
cǫnta	rǫmpe
contǎmos	rompẹmos
(contǎis)	(rompẹis)
cǫntam	rǫmpem

b) In verbs of the first conjugation, if radical o is followed by
l + consonant, it is pronounced ǫ when accented and ǫ when
unaccented.

vǫlto   voltạmos
(vǫltas)   (voltạis)
vǫlta   vǫltam

**113. Radical-changing verbs. Verbs of the third conjugation with
radical *u*.**

subo   subimos
(sǫbes)   (subis)
sǫbe   sǫbem

VOCABULARY

apressạr-se to hurry
a beira-mạr the seashore
o cheiro the odor
despir-se to undress
dever to owe; to have to, must
divertir-se to enjoy oneself
dormir to sleep
estạr de vǫlta to be back
o fạto de banho the bathing suit; *see*
 roupa de banho *below*
ficạr contente (em) to be glad (to)
levạr to take (away)
morrer to die; morrer de to die of
 languish with
o pacǫte the package

pôr to put on
a praia the beach
pronto -a ready
o quạrto de dormir the bedroom
a roupa de banho (*Brazilian*) bathing
 suit
sentạr-se to sit down, seat oneself
sentir to smell
subir to go up
o tio the uncle
tomạr to get, take
tomạr um banho de mạr to go bathing
 in the ocean
vestir to put on
vestir-se to dress (oneself)

EXERCISES

A. *Read.* João—Não quer você ir à beira-mar comigo tomar
um banho de mar?

José—Quero, muito obrigado, fico contente em ir consigo (*Bra-zilian:* com você). Divirto-me sempre à beira-mar. A que horas
deseja partir?

João—Você está pronto a partir?

José—Sim, estou. Devemos apressar-nos?

João—Podemos tomar o combóio (*Brazilian:* trem) das onze.
Iremos a casa de meu tio que mora perto da praia. Levaremos os
nossos fatos (*Brazilian:* roupas) de banho connosco. Poderemos
vesti-los (*Brazilian:* -las *for* roupas de banho) em casa do meu tio.
Passaremos a tarde na praia e estaremos de volta às cinco.

José—Pois, vamo-nos (*let's go*), estou pronto.

B. *Answer in Portuguese.* 1. José quer ir à beira-mar com
João? 2. Diverte-se José à beira-mar? 3. A que horas devem
partir? 4. Devem apressar-se? 5. Onde mora o tio de João? 6.
Alugam os rapazes fatos (*Brazilian:* roupas) de banho? 7. Porquê
vão a casa do tio de João? 8. A que horas contam estar de volta?

C. *Translate the English words to complete the sentence.* 1. O
senhor *owe me* dinheiro. 2. Êles *sleep* tarde. 3. *Put on* o fato
(*Brazilian:* a roupa) de banho. 4. Êle *is going up* ao quarto de
dormir. 5. Vá à livraria *to get* os meus livros. 6. Eu *take* o combóio (*Brazilian:* trem) tôdas as manhãs às nove. 7. Eu sempre
enjoy myself em Nova York. 8. Eu *shall get* os livros e *take them*
comigo. 9. *Take* êsse pacote consigo. 10. Eu *sleep* nesta cama.

D. *Translate.* 1. Divirto-me sempre à beira-mar. 2. Leve[1]
êste pacote ao seu amigo. 3. Vestiu-se esta manhã muito cedo.
4. Dispo-me e leio na cama antes de adormecer. 5. João vestia o
fato (*Brazilian:* a roupa) de banho quando seu pai o chamou.
6. Tirou o chapéu quando entrou no quarto. 7. Divertir-nos-emos
muito em Nova York na próxima semana. 8. Sentámo-nos à
mesa às sete. 9. O senhor deve trabalhar esta tarde? 10. Sim,
devo. 11. Apressam-se porque devem estar de volta antes das
seis. 12. Sinto o cheiro das flores no jardim. 13. Deve-me muito
dinheiro.

E. *Translate.* 1. Vou à biblioteca tomar um livro. 2. Have-
mos-de tomar o combóio (*Brazilian:* trem) às nove e um quarto.
3. Subimos ao quarto de dormir às dez e deitámo-nos às dez e

---

[1] Command form of **levar.**

meia. 4. Dormiu bem a noite passada? 5. Sim, dormi muito bem e não acordei antes das oito. 6. Acordo geralmente cedo. 7. Dormíamos quando êle se foi embora. 8. Sobe ao seu quarto agora? 9. Sim, subo. 10. Morro de fome. 11. Morria de sêde. 12. Pus o chapéu.

F. *Translate.* 1. I got a book this morning at the bookstore. 2. I shall take the train to go to the seashore. 3. Are you dressing now? 4. Yes, I am dressing. 5. We are hurrying because we must be back at three o'clock. 6. I always enjoy myself at the theater. 7. Put on your hat and come with me. 8. We shall put on our bathing suits. 9. Come up to my room at once. 10. I was dressing in my bedroom when he called me. 11. I get awake at six o'clock every morning. 12. He took that package to the station. 13. He got this package at the station. 14. I owe them money.

Lesson XVIII

114. Conjugation of *pedir* *to ask, request.* Although **pedir** is a radical-changing verb, it does not have a radical change in the first singular present indicative but is irregular in this form.

pẹço	pedịmos
pẹdes	pedịs
pẹde	pẹdem

115. Present subjunctive. The stem of the present subjunctive is found by dropping the ending **o** of the first singular present indicative.[1]

1st sg. pres. ind.	fạl-o	aprẹnd-o	pạrt-o
	SINGULAR	SINGULAR	SINGULAR
1.	fạl-e	aprẹnd-a	pạrt-a
2.	(fạl-es)	(aprẹnd-as)	(pạrt-as)
3.	fạl-e	aprẹnd-a	pạrt-a
	PLURAL	PLURAL	PLURAL
1.	fal-ẹmos	aprend-ạmos	part-ạmos
2.	(fal-ẹis)	(aprend-ạis)	(part-ạis)
3.	fạl-em	aprẹnd-am	pạrt-am

a) The stem of the present subjunctive of radical-changing verbs is found in the same way, the radical vowel being the same as that of the first singular present indicative. Note, however, that in the first and second plural of verbs of the first and second conjugations radical **e** is pronounced like French mute *e* and radical **o** is pronounced like *u* in *rule*.

1st sg. pres. ind.	lẹv-o	dẹv-o	sịrv-o
	SINGULAR	SINGULAR	SINGULAR
1.	lẹv-e	dẹv-a	sịrv-a
2.	(lẹv-es)	(dẹv-as)	(sịrv-as)
3.	lẹv-e	dẹv-a	sịrv-a

[1] It is clear now that the command forms (section 87) are the third singular and plural forms of the present subjunctive. The first plural present subjunctive is similarly used and is equivalent to English *let us . . .* : **Falemos português** *Let us speak Portuguese.*

84

	PLURAL	PLURAL	PLURAL
1.	lev-emos	dev-amos	sirv-amos
2.	(lev-eis)	(dev-ais)	(sirv-ais)
3.	lev-em	dev-am	sirv-am

| 1st sg. pres. ind. | tom-o | mov-o | durm-o |

	SINGULAR	SINGULAR	SINGULAR
1.	tom-e	mov-a	durm-a
2.	(tom-es)	(mov-as)	(durm-as)
3.	tom-e	mov-a	durm-a

	PLURAL	PLURAL	PLURAL
1.	tom-emos	mov-amos	durm-amos
2.	(tom-eis)	(mov-ais)	(durm-ais)
3.	tom-em	mov-am	durm-am

116. Use of subjunctive. The subjunctive is used in noun clauses introduced by **que** after verbs expressing wish, preference, command, request, advice, insistence, permission, consent, approval, prohibition, and similar ideas.

Desejo que se levante cedo.   *I want you to get up early.*
Mando que parta.   *I am ordering you to go away.*

a) If the subject of the dependent verb is the same as the subject of the main verb, the infinitive is used.

Desejo levantar-me cedo.   *I want to get up early.*

b) After some verbs the subjunctive and the infinitive may be used interchangeably.

Profbo-lhe que venha.
Profbo-lhe vir.   *I forbid him to come.*

c) After **pedir** an infinitive is preceded by the preposition **para**.

Pede para ver a casa.   *He asks to see the house.*

d) After the verb **dizer** implying command, only the subjunctive may be used.

Digo-lhe que espere.   *I tell him to wait.*

VOCABULARY

aconselhar (a que) to advise
beber to drink
o cachimbo the pipe
a cadeira the chair
o charuto the cigar
o cigarro the cigarette
comer to eat
conveniente convenient
deixar to let, allow; deixar de to stop, cease
escrever to write
a esquina the corner
a filha the daughter
o filho the son

a frase the sentence
fumar to smoke
mandar to order
mover to move
o pai the father
pedir to ask, request
permitir to permit, let
preferir to prefer
proïbir to prohibit, forbid
repetir to repeat
o sêlo do correio the postage stamp
a tabacaria the cigar store
tossir to cough

EXERCISES

A. *Read.* —Meu pai deseja que eu compre um cachimbo para êle. O médico aconselha-lhe a que deixe de fumar charutos e cigarros. Onde se pode achar uma tabacaria?

—Há uma boa tabacaria na esquina da rua.

—E onde posso comprar jornais?

—O senhor pode comprar jornais também na tabacaria. Em Portugal vendem-se jornais e selos do correio nas tabacarias.

—Muito obrigado, não sabia isso. É muito conveniente.

B. *Answer in Portuguese.* 1. O que deseja seu pai que compre para êle? 2. Porquê deseja um cachimbo? 3. Onde há uma boa tabacaria? 4. Onde se pode comprar jornais? selos do correio? 5. Não sabia o senhor que vendiam jornais nas tabacarias?

C. *Translate the English words to complete the sentence.* 1. Desejo que o senhor *write* uma carta a meu irmão. 2. Digo-lhe *not to smoke* tanto. 3. Peço-lhe que *come* já. 4. Aconselho-lhe a que *go away.* 5. Mandá-lo-ei *to work* muito. 6. Quere que o filho *learn* o português. 7. Aconselha-nos a que não *eat* tanto. 8. Essa água não é boa, *don't drink it.* 9. Prefiro que *you speak* mais devagar. 10. *Don't cough* tanto.

D. *Translate.* 1. O senhor deseja que trabalhemos todo o dia. 2. Êle aconselha-nos a que estudemos muito. 3. Não nos deixa comer antes das nove. 4. Ela diz que falemos de-vagar. 5. Não deixa que o filho fume. 6. Mandamos que todos se levantem cedo àmanhã. 7. Aconselho-lhe a não beber essa água. 8. Mando que os alunos se deitem antes das dez e meia. 9. Queremos que aprendam bem as suas lições. 10. Pedem que estudemos muito. 11. O médico aconselha-me a não fumar. 12. Pede-me que estude muito.

E. *Translate.* 1. Proïbimos que durma tarde. 2. Quero que tomem na loja um pacote para mim. 3. Não permite que se mova a cadeira. 4. Não coma tanto. 5. Quero que não beba tanto vinho. 6. Deseja que a filha me escreva uma carta tôdas as semanas. 7. O médico diz que eu não beba tanto vinho. 8. O professor diz que repitamos a frase. 9. A nossa mãe quer que nos vistamos cedo. 10. Desejam que não tussamos tanto. 11. Queremos que os senhores se divirtam hoje. 12. Quero que se apressem. 13. Peço que repita a frase. 14. Permita o senhor que João mova a cadeira. 15. Dir-lhe-ei que tome um bilhete para mim.

F. *Translate.* 1. We want you to work hard. 2. Do not drink that wine. 3. He advises us to study Portuguese. 4. We do not allow them to smoke. 5. He orders us to go to bed. 6. They ask us to hurry. 7. I tell him not to cough so much. 8. I do not allow those chairs to be moved. 9. I want you to enjoy yourself here. 10. I wish to write her a letter, and I wish you to write her a letter too. 11. Let the boy write a letter to his friend.

Lesson XIX

117. Present subjunctive (continued). The stem of the present subjunctive of irregular verbs is found in the same way as that of other verbs (section 115), with the following exceptions.

a) Seven irregular verbs have an irregular stem in the whole present subjunctive. Note that the pronunciation of the radical vowel of the first and second plural of **estar** and **ser** changes according to section 111 b.

Inf.	dạr	estạr	sẹr	ịr	havẹr	sabẹr	querẹr
1st sg. pres. ind.	dọu	estọu	sọu	vọu	hẹi	sẹi	quẹro
Pres. subj.	dê	estẹja	sẹja	vá	hạja	sạiba	quẹira
	(dês)	(estẹjas)	(sẹjas)	(vás)	(hạjas)	(sạibas)	(quẹiras)
	dê	estẹja	sẹja	vá	hạja	sạiba	quẹira
	dêmos	estejạmos	sejạmos	vạmos	hajạmos	saibạmos	queirạmos
	(dẹis)	(estejạis)	(sejạis)	(vạdes)	(hajạis)	(saibạis)	(queirạis)
	dêem	estẹjam	sẹjam	vão	hạjam	sạibam	quẹiram

b) Two irregular verbs have an irregular stem in the first and second plural present subjunctive.

Inf.	crẹr		lẹr	
1st sg. pres. ind.	crẹio		lẹio	
Pres. subj.	crẹia		lẹia	
	(crẹias)		(lẹias)	
	crẹia		lẹia	
	creạmos	(e = y)	leạmos	(e = y)
	(creạis)	(e = y)	(leạis)	(e = y)
	crẹiam		lẹiam	

c) Four more irregular verbs have a change in the pronunciation of the radical vowel in the first and second plural present subjunctive (three of them according to section 111 b).

Inf.	ter	vir	ver	pôr
1st sg. pres. ind.	tenho	venho	vejo	ponho
Pres. subj.	tenha	venha	veja	ponha
	(tenhas)	(venhas)	(vejas)	(ponhas)
	tenha	venha	veja	ponha
	tenhamos	venhamos	vejamos	ponhamos
	(tenhais)	(venhais)	(vejais)	(ponhais)
	tenham	venham	vejam	ponham

118. Use of subjunctive (continued). 1. The subjunctive is used in noun clauses introduced by **que** after verbs expressing emotion (such as joy, sorrow, hope, fear, surprise).

Fico contente que venha.	*I am glad that he is coming.*
Sinto que esteja doente.	*I am sorry that you are ill.*

a) The verb **esperar** *to hope* may be followed by the indicative if probability of realisation of the hope is implied.

Espero que virá.	*I hope that he will come.*

b) If the subject of the dependent verb is the same as the subject of the main verb, the infinitive is used.

Sinto não poder ir.	*I am sorry that I cannot go.*

2. The subjunctive is used in noun clauses introduced by **que** after verbs expressing doubt or disbelief.

Não creio que esteja aqui.	*I do not believe that he is here.*
Duvido que fale português.	*I doubt if he speaks Portuguese.*

a) If these verbs express or imply belief, the indicative is used.

Não crê que está aqui?	*Do you not believe that he is here?*
Não duvido que fala português bem.	*I do not doubt that he speaks Portuguese well.*

3. The subjunctive is used in noun clauses introduced by **que** after impersonal verbs (usually **ser** plus a noun or an adjective) that do not express certainty or probability.

É possível que o faça.	*It is possible he will do it.*
É tempo que êle se vá.	*It is time for him to leave.*
É preciso que partamos.	*It is necessary that we leave.*

a) If the impersonal verb expresses certainty, the indicative is used.

É certo que virá.	*It is sure that he will come.*
É verdade que mora aqui.	*It is true that he lives here.*

VOCABULARY

abęrto -a open
alęgre gay, merry
além de besides
algụm, algụma some
apresentạr to introduce
assegurạr to assure, guarantee
o clịma the climate
a companhịa the company
contẹnte (de) content, satisfied, glad (to)
delicịoso delightful
doẹnte sick, ill
duvidạr to doubt

a espécie the kind
esperạr to hope, wait for
a estaçạo balnẹar the bathing resort
gozạr to enjoy
mụitas vẹzes often
é pẹna que it is a pity that
provável probable
sentịr to be sorry
surpreendẹr to surprise; surpreẹnde-me I am surprised
temẹr to fear
tẹr pẹna to be sorry
vạmos + *infinitive* let us . . .

EXERCISES

A. *Read.*   Fico contente que o senhor Martins vá passar algum tempo êste verão em Lisboa.   Asseguro que vai divertir-se muito. Tenho muitos amigos alegres a quem apresentá-lo.   E além da boa companhia poderá gozar os teatros e cinemas, que estão abertos todas as noites.   Espero que irá muitas vezes ao Estoril para tomar banhos de mar.   O Estoril é uma estação balnear e o seu clima é delicioso.

B. *Answer in Portuguese.*   1. Você fica contente que o senhor Martins vá passar algum tempo em Lisboa?   2. Você crê que há de divertir-se em Lisboa?   3. Apresentá-lo-á aos seus amigos?   4. Você tem muitos amigos em Lisboa?   5. Estão abertos os cinemas

de Lisboa no verão? 6. Porquê irá o senhor Martins ao Estoril?
7. O que é o Estoril? 8. Que espécie de clima tem?

C. *Translate the English words to complete the sentence.* 1. Tenho
pena que seu irmão *is* doente. 2. Fico contente que o senhor *will
come* ver-nos. 3. Duvido que êles *know* o nome do senhor. 4. É
possível que êle *will read* a notícia no jornal. 5. É pena que João *is
not* aqui. 6. Aconselho-lhes a que *take a walk* no parque. 7. Não
estou certo que João *has* os livros. 8. Sinto muitíssimo que os
senhores *cannot* ler o espanhol. 9. Quero *you to see* a minha casa.
10. Quero *to see* a sua casa.

D. *Translate.* 1. Prefiro que se vão imediatamente. 2. Queremos que nos dê o dinheiro. 3. João deseja que venhamos imediatamente. 4. Quer que o filho diga sempre a verdade. 5. Aconse-
lham a que estejamos contentes de ficar nesta cidade. 6. Quero que
saibam a verdade. 7. Proíbem que dêmos um passeio no jardim.
8. Quero ir-me embora mas não quero que êle se vá. 9. Manda que
os alunos dêem os jornais aos pais. 10. Êles querem que vejamos
a sua casa. 11. Pede que leamos o jornal todos os dias. 12.
Queremos que ponha a cadeira atrás da mesa. 13. Dizem que
ponhamos os livros sôbre a mesa. 14. Peço-lhe para vir ver-me.

E. *Translate.* 1. Sentimos que o senhor não possa vir ver-nos.
2. Surpreende-me que êle não venha hoje. 3. Crê o senhor que o
professor venha cedo? 4. Não creio que venha cedo. 5. Não é
provável que João aprenda o português em tão pouco tempo. 6. É
preciso que estudemos muito. 7. Esperamos estar aqui àmanhã.
8. Temo que os alunos não saibam a lição. 9. Não é certo que
João venha. 10. Ficamos contentes que não estejam doentes. 11.
Tenho pena que o professor não venha hoje. 12. É certo que João
me dará o seu livro. 13. Preferimos que o senhor fale francês.
14. É pena que não possamos ficar. 15. Vamos comer. 16. Vamos enviar-lhe a carta.

F. *Translate.* 1. I want you to tell me the truth. 2. He orders
us to give the newspapers to the pupils. 3. I ask him to go away.

4. We advise you to read the newspapers.   **5.** He is sorry that you will not get up early.   **6.** It is necessary for you to go to bed at once. **7.** She is glad that you are studying Portuguese.   **8.** I am surprised that you do not speak English.   **9.** He does not believe that I read Portuguese.   **10.** His father wants him to learn Portuguese.   **11.** We do not doubt that you know your lesson.   **12.** It is true that he is working hard.   **13.** I am afraid that John will not come.   **14.** We hope that he will be here tomorrow.   **15.** Let us drink all the wine.   **16.** He is surprised that I do not speak Spanish.

Lesson XX

119. Orthographic-changing verbs. In order to make the spelling correctly represent the unchanging sound of a stem ending, it is necessary to change

c (hard) to **qu** before **e**

	PRETERIT	PRES. SUBJ.
ficar:	fiquei, ficaste, etc.	fique, fiques, etc.

g (hard) to **gu** before **e**

	PRETERIT	PRES. SUBJ.
chegar [1]:	cheguei, chegaste, etc.	chegue, chegues, etc.

g (soft) to **j** before **o** and **a**

	PRES. IND.	PRES. SUBJ.
corrigir:	corrijo, corriges, etc.	corrija, corrijas, etc.

gu to **g** before **o** and **a**

	PRES. IND.	PRES. SUBJ.
seguir [2]:	sigo, segues, etc.	siga, sigas, etc.

ç to **c** before **e**

	PRETERIT	PRES. SUBJ.
começar:	comecei, começaste, etc.	comece, comeces, etc.

c to **ç** before **o** and **a**

	PRES. IND.	PRES. SUBJ.
esquecer [3]:	esqueço, esqueces, etc.	esqueça, esqueças, etc.

[1] The radical **e** of **chegar** is always pronounced **ę** when accented and like *i* in *perish* when unaccented.

[2] Note that **seguir** is also a radical-changing verb conjugated like **servir**.

[3] Note that the radical **e** (the second **e**) of **esquecer** is pronounced **ę** when unaccented and not like French mute *e*.

93

120. Future subjunctive. The future subjunctive is formed by dropping the last syllable **-ram** of the third plural preterit indicative and adding **-r, -res, -r, -rmos, -rdes, -rem.**

Inf.	falạr	aprendẹr	partịr	dizẹr	sẹr and ịr
3d pl. pret. ind.	falạ-ram	aprendẹ-ram	partị-ram	dissẹ-ram	fọ-ram
Future subj.	falạ-r	aprendẹ-r	partị-r	dissẹ-r	fọ-r
	falạ-res	aprendẹ-res	partị-res	dissẹ-res	fọ-res
	falạ-r	aprendẹ-r	partị-r	dissẹ-r	fọ-r
	falạ-rmos	aprendẹ-rmos	partị-rmos	dissẹ-rmos	fọ-rmos
	falạ-rdes	aprendẹ-rdes	partị-rdes	dissẹ-rdes	fọ-rdes
	falạ-rem	aprendẹ-rem	partị-rem	dissẹ-rem	fọ-rem

121. Use of subjunctive (continued). The subjunctive is used in adverbial clauses introduced by certain subordinating conjunctions.

1. Conjunctions of time requiring the subjunctive when the verb refers to the future.

quạndo	*when*	enquạnto (que)	*while*
ạntes que	*before*	ao pạsso que	*while*
depọis que	*after*	lọgo que	*as soon as*
até que	*until*	assịm que	*as soon as*

Estarei aqui até que acabe o tra-   *I shall be here until he finishes the work.*
balho.

a) The future subjunctive is generally used instead of the present subjunctive after **quando, enquanto (que), assim que, logo que,** and **depois que.**

Ir-me-ei embora quando chegar.   *I shall leave when he arrives.*

2. Conjunctions of concession requiring the subjunctive when the verb does not state an accomplished fact.

ạinda que	*although*	embọra	*although*
pôsto que	*although*		

Não saïrei ainda que não chova.   *I shall not go out although it may not rain.*

a) In Brazilian Portuguese, conjunctions of concession always require the subjunctive.

3. Conjunctions of condition, denial, and purpose requiring the subjunctive.

CONDITION		DENIAL	
contanto que	*provided (that)*	sem que	*without*
sempre que	*provided (that)*		PURPOSE
(no) caso (que)	*in case (that)*	para que	*so that, in order that*
a menos que	*unless*	a-fim que	*so that, in order that*
a não ser que	*unless*	de modo que	*so that*

Dar-lhe-ei o dinheiro contanto que faça o trabalho. — *I shall give him the money provided he does the work.*

Irei sem que êle o saiba. — *I shall go without his knowing it.*

Dar-lhe-ei um guarda-chuva para que não se molhe. — *I shall give you an umbrella so that you will not get wet.*

a) When result rather than purpose is expressed, the indicative is used.

Dei-lhe um guarda-chuva de modo que não se molhou. — *I gave you an umbrella so that (with the result that) you did not get wet.*

VOCABULARY

a alfaiataria the tailor shop
o alfaiate the tailor
a amostra the sample
o automóvel the automobile
o bonde (*Brazilian*) the trolley car
os carris de ferro trolley lines; *see* linhas de bonde *below*
o carro eléctrico the trolley car; *see* bonde *above*
chegar to arrive; chegar a casa to arrive home
chover to rain
conhecer to know
conseguir to get, obtain
a conta the bill
a côr the color
corrigir to correct
descer to go down; to get off; descer de to get off *or* out of (*a vehicle*)
diferente different
direito (*adv.*) straight
a escada the stairs
esquecer(-se de) to forget
a estação final (*Brazilian*) the terminus
o exemplo the example

o exercício the exercise
o fato the suit (of clothes); *see* terno *below*
a fazenda the cloth
o ferro the iron
igual a like, similar to
ir a pé to walk
a lã the wool
lembrar-se de to remember
levar to wear
as linhas de bonde (*Brazilian*) trolley lines
mostrar to show
pagar to pay
a paragem central the terminus; *see* estação final *above*
o pé the foot
pouco -a little
a praça the public square
a prova the proof
seguir to follow
subir to go up, come up; subir para to get on *or* into (*a vehicle*)
o terno (*Brazilian*) the suit (of clothes)
voltar para casa to return home

EXERCISES

A. *Read.* José—Você não quer que comamos no hotel antes de ir às compras (*Brazilian:* fazer compras)?

João—Irei consigo (*Brazilian:* com você) tomar alguma coisa, ainda que estou (*Brazilian:* esteja) com pouca vontade de comer.

José—Depois que comermos, levá-lo-ei à alfaiataria da rua do Carmo. Quero que o alfaiate me dê amostras de lã igual à fazenda dêste fato (*Brazilian:* terno) que levo mas de côres diferentes.

João—Iremos a pé ou tomaremos o carro eléctrico (*Brazilian:* bonde)?

José—Iremos a pé a menos que chova. Quando tomo o carro eléctrico (*Brazilian:* bonde), desço no Rossio. Sabe que o Rossio é a paragem central (*Brazilian:* estação final) dos carris de ferro (*Brazilian:* linhas de bonde)? É uma praça.

B. *Answer in Portuguese.* 1. O que quer fazer José antes que os rapazes vão às compras (*Brazilian:* fazer compras)? 2. João está com fome? 3. Para onde vão na rua do Carmo? 4. O que deseja José fazer ali? 5. Irão os rapazes a pé à rua do Carmo? 6. O que é o Rossio?

C. *Translate the English words to complete the sentence.* 1. Estará aqui quando nós *arrive.* 2. Virei àmanhã caso *the weather is good.* 3. Não aprende muito ainda que *he studies* muito. 4. Desejo *you to follow me* no seu automóvel. 5. Ir-se-ão sem que *our knowing it.* 6. Virá ver-me àmanhã a menos que *he forgets.* 7. Deitar-se-á depois que *he eats.* 8. Conseguirá os livros contanto que *he pays* a conta. 9. Darei dinheiro a João para que *he can* tomar o carro eléctrico (*Brazilian:* bonde). 10. Chamarei você assim que o médico *arrives.*

D. *Translate.* 1. Êle deseja que fiquemos em casa. 2. Cheguei a casa muito tarde. 3. Corrijo as provas do meu livro. 4. Levante-se cedo e siga o exemplo dos meus alunos. 5. Aconselham-nos a que comecemos a preparar a nossa lição para àmanhã. 6. O professor diz que não esqueçamos os nossos livros. 7. Quero que desçam a escada imediatamente. 8. Conheço todos os seus amigos.

9. Quer que paguemos o dinheiro que devemos. 10. Desça do automóvel e suba para o carro eléctrico (*Brazilian:* bonde).

E. *Translate.* 1. Fico em casa até que deixe de chover. 2. Escreva-me uma carta assim que voltar. 3. Não vou ao teatro a menos que o senhor vá comigo. 4. Depois que terminar o livro, dar-lho-ei. 5. Caso chova, não poderemos dar um passeio. 6. Pagar-lhe-emos, contanto que termine o trabalho hoje. 7. Os alunos não aprendem muito a menos que corrijamos os exercícios. 8. Não podemos partir sem que o permitam. 9. Logo que descermos do carro eléctrico (*Brazilian:* bonde), iremos para a praia. 10. Subimos a escada para que João nos mostre a sua biblioteca. 11. Não aprenderá o inglês ainda que estude muito. 12. Diga-lhe que venha ver-me, caso se lembre de mim. 13. Deitar-se-á assim que voltar para casa.

F. *Translate.* 1. Tell John to go straight to the station as soon as his sister gets out of the automobile. 2. He does not learn English, although he studies it a great deal. 3. I want you to follow the example of my pupils when you study Portuguese. 4. He will not go to bed early, although he arrives home before ten o'clock. 5. Unless you remember your lesson, they will not allow you to go to the theater. 6. In case the weather is fine, he will take a walk in the garden. 7. They will tell the truth provided they know you. 8. It will not be a good book unless you correct the proofs. 9. I shall repeat those sentences so that you do not forget them. 10. He will come up to see you as soon as he returns. 11. I cannot show him my books unless he arrives before six o'clock. 12. He will learn to write Portuguese provided he does the exercises of each lesson.

Lesson XXI

122. Conjugation of *perder* *to lose, miss.* Although **perder** is a radical-changing verb, it does not have a radical change in the first singular present indicative but is irregular in this form.

pẹrco	perdẹmos
(pẹrdes)	(perdẹis)
pẹrde	pẹrdem

The present subjunctive is, of course, derived in the regular way from the first singular present indicative: **pẹrca, pẹrcas,** etc.

123. Imperfect subjunctive. The imperfect subjunctive is formed by dropping the last syllable, **-ram,** of the third plural preterit indicative and adding **-sse, -sses, -sse, -ssemos, -sseis, -ssem.** The vowel preceding **-ssemos** and **-sseis** takes a written accent. This accent is acute in all verbs except regular verbs of the second conjugation and **ser** (and **ir**), where it is circumflex.

Inf.	**falạr**	**aprendẹr**	**partịr**	**dizẹr**	**sẹr** and **ịr**
3d pl. pret. ind.	falạ-ram	aprendẹ-ram	partị-ram	dissẹ-ram	fọ-ram
Imperf.subj.	falạ-sse	aprendẹ-sse	partị-sse	dissẹ-sse	fọ-sse
	(falạ-sses)	(aprendẹ-sses)	(partị-sses)	(dissẹ-sses)	(fọ-sses)
	falạ-sse	aprendẹ-sse	partị-sse	dissẹ-sse	fọ-sse
	falá-ssemos	aprendê-ssemos	partí-ssemos	dissé-ssemos	fô-ssemos
	(falá-sseis)	(aprendê-sseis)	(partí-sseis)	(dissé-sseis)	(fô-sseis)
	falạ-ssem	aprendẹ-ssem	partị-ssem	dissẹ-ssem	fọ-ssem

124. Sequence of tenses. 1. If the main verb of a sentence is in the present tense, a dependent subjunctive is in the present if it refers to the present or the future, in the imperfect if it refers to the past.

Sinto muito que não venha.	*I am sorry he is not coming* (or *will not come*).
Sinto muito que não viesse.	*I am sorry he did not come.*

2. If the main verb of a sentence is in any past tense, a dependent subjunctive is generally in the imperfect.[1]

Disse-lhe que falasse português. *I told him to speak Portuguese.*

125. Use of subjunctive (continued). The subjunctive is used in adjective clauses introduced by a relative pronoun to indicate that the antecedent is indefinite or nonexistent.

Procuro uma criada que fale francês. *I am looking for a maid who speaks French.*

Não conheço ninguém aqui que fale português. *I do not know anyone here who speaks Portuguese.*

a) The future subjunctive is sometimes used instead of the present in adjective clauses of this kind.

Tôda a pessoa que chegar antes das oito fica convidada a jantar. *Any person who arrives before eight o'clock is invited to dinner.*

VOCABULARY

acomodar-se to adapt oneself
antes (*adv.*) before
assim so, thus
o brasileiro[2] the Brazilian; **brasileiro -a** Brazilian
cantar to sing
o chá the tea
o costume the custom
encetar to begin; to establish
encontrar to meet; to find
ensinar to teach
a Espanha Spain
fàcilmente easily
gostar de to like

o guarda-chuva the umbrella
ninguém no one, nobody
perder to lose, miss
porém however
procurar to try; to look for, seek
quanto antes as soon as possible
a relação the relation, the contact
ter pressa (de) to be in a hurry (to)
ir ter com to go to, go to see, apply to
vir ter com to come to, come to see, apply to
viajar to travel
a vida the life
vir a to come to, happen to

[1] If the time of the dependent subjunctive is prior to the time of the main verb, the pluperfect subjunctive (**tivesse** + past participle) may be used, e.g., **Senti que não tivesse vindo** *I was sorry that he had not come.*

[2] Adjectives of nationality are not capitalized in Portuguese when used as nouns.

EXERCISES

A. *Read.* O meu pai desejou que aprendêssemos o português quando éramos jovens. Procurou um brasileiro que pudesse ensinar-nos a língua. Assim é que viemos a conhecer o senhor Martins. Além de ensinar-nos a língua, contou-nos muita coisa sôbre a vida brasileira. É pena que não fôssemos antes ao Brasil. Estou certo porém que quando lá formos, poderemos acomodar-nos muito fàcilmente aos costumes brasileiros. Logo que chegarmos ao Rio, procuraremos encetar boas relações com todos os brasileiros que encontrarmos.

B. *Answer in Portuguese.* 1. Como é que os senhores aprenderam o português quando eram jovens? 2. Quem lhes ensinou o português? 3. Sabem alguma coisa sôbre a vida brasileira? 4. Contam acomodar-se fàcilmente aos costumes brasileiros? 5. O que vão fazer logo que chegarem ao Rio?

C. *Translate the English words to complete the sentence.* 1. Não havia ninguém na loja que *spoke* inglês. 2. Eu temia que o senhor *would not come.* 3. Fico contente que *he did not miss* o combóio (*Brazilian:* trem). 4. Desejava *you to write me* uma carta. 5. Trouxe-lhe um lápis para que *you would be able* escrever os exercícios. 6. Sentia muito que o senhor *did not know* o meu amigo. 7. Eu disse a João *to come up* ao meu quarto. 8. Procurava um professor que *could* ensinar-me o português. 9. Eu não acreditava que êle *would come.* 10. Ficava contente que você *were learning* o português.

D. *Translate.* 1. Perdeu muito dinheiro o ano passado. 2. Aconselho-lhe a que não perca o combóio (*Brazilian:* trem) das oito. 3. Fui ter com o professor para saber o número da próxima lição. 4. Gosta o senhor de chá? 5. Sim, senhor, gosto. 6. Gostamos de viajar. 7. Temos pressa de terminar êsse trabalho. 8. Sempre tem grande pressa. 9. Hei-de vir ter consigo (*Brazilian:* com o senhor) àmanhã. 10. Gosto muito de Lisboa. 11. Não se apresse tanto. 12. Encontrei êste lápis no seu quarto. 13. Fêz uma viagem à Espanha.

E. *Translate.* 1. Desejava que viesse ver-me ontem. 2. Aconselharam-nos a que nos vestíssemos imediatamente. 3. Não permiti que bebessem essa água. 4. O médico disse que não bebêssemos tanto vinho. 5. Não acreditei que o fizesse. 6. Queria que pagássemos o dinheiro que devíamos. 7. Levei o guarda-chuva, caso que chovesse. 8. Êle não queria cantar ainda que fosse feliz. 9. Fico muito contente que êle se fosse embora. 10. Disse-lho para que soubesse a verdade. 11. Foi-se embora sem que ninguém o visse. 12. João sentiu que não pudéssemos vir esta manhã. 13. Mandaram que fôssemos ter com o professor àmanhã. 14. Tinha pressa de lhe dizer que viesse quanto antes. 15. Não havia ninguém ali que me conhecesse. 16. Procuro um professor que me ensine o português.

F. *Translate.* 1. I did not want you to miss the train. 2. The doctor told us not to eat so much. 3. They wanted us to tell them the truth. 4. No one could enter the city without his permitting it. 5. He did not like to sing because he was not happy. 6. They did not allow me to go to see the professor. 7. He would not take tea, although he was very tired. 8. They ordered us to finish our work as soon as possible. 9. I told him to go to see the doctor at once. 10. He advised me to travel. 11. I am glad that he took an umbrella with him when he went to the theater. 12. We were afraid that you would miss the train. 13. We were looking for a man who could speak Spanish.

Lesson XXII

126. Present indicative of *ouvir* *to hear* **and** *cair* *to fall.*

ouço and oiço	caio
ouves	cais
ouve	cai
ouvimos	caímos
ouvis	caís
ouvem	caem

The verb **sair** *to go out* is conjugated like **cair**.

127. Conditional. The conditional is formed by adding to the infinitive the endings **-ia, -ias, -ia, -íamos, -íeis,** and **-iam.**

falaria	falaríamos
(falarias)	(falaríeis)
falaria	falariam

a) The conditionals of the verbs **dizer, fazer,** and **trazer** are formed on shortened infinitives: **diria, faria,** and **traria.** See section 103 a.

b) The position of pronouns with the conditional is the same as their position with the simple future (section 104).

128. Conditional sentences. Conditional sentences are made up of two parts, an if-clause, which is the dependent clause, and a conclusion, which is independent and contains the main verb.

1. When the if-clause refers to the present or past and is not contrary to fact, the indicative is used in both parts of the sentence and there is no special construction to be learned.

Se tem dinheiro, dá-mo. *If he has any money, he gives it to me.*
Se veio ontem à noite, não o sabia. *If he came last night, I did not know it.*

2. When the if-clause expresses pure condition in the future, the present indicative or the future subjunctive is used in the if-clause and the future indicative in the conclusion.

Se vem ver-me, falar-lhe-ei.⎫
Se vier ver-me, falar-lhe-ei.⎭ *If he comes to see me, I shall speak to him.*

102

3. When the if-clause expresses doubtful condition in the future, the imperfect subjunctive is used in the if-clause and the imperfect indicative (or the conditional in literary and more formal Portuguese) in the conclusion.

Se viesse ver-me, falava-lhe (or **falar-lhe-ia**). — *If he should come to see me, I should speak to him.*

a) The imperfect indicative may be used also in the softened expression of a wish and in a conclusion without an if-clause.

Desejava estudar o espanhol. — *I should like to study Spanish.*
Podia emprestar-lhe o dinheiro. — *I could lend you the money.*

4. When the if-clause expresses condition contrary to fact, the imperfect subjunctive is used in the if-clause and the imperfect indicative (or the conditional in literary and more formal Portuguese) in the conclusion.

Se tivesse o dinheiro, fazia (or **faria**) **uma viagem ao Brasil êste ano.** — *If I had the money, I should take a trip to Brazil this year.*

a) The same construction may be used if the time is past, although the corresponding compound tenses are considered more grammatical.

Se tivesse o dinheiro, fazia (or **faria**) **uma viagem ao Brasil o ano passado.** — *If I had the money, I should have taken a trip to Brazil last year.*

5. The word **se** meaning *whether* does not take the subjunctive.

Não sei se veio. — *I do not know whether he came.*
Não sei se virá. — *I do not know whether he will come.*

a) The imperfect indicative may be used instead of the conditional with **se** meaning *whether.*

Não sabia se vinha (or **viria**). — *I did not know whether he would come.*

129. Negatives.

ninguém	nobody, no one	nada	nothing, not anything
nenhum, nenhuma, nenhuns, nenhumas	no, not any	nunca	never
		nem . . . nem	neither . . . nor

When these negatives follow the verb, **não** must precede it.

Ninguém estava ali. ⎱
Não estava ali ninguém. ⎰   *No one was there.*

VOCABULARY

aceitar to accept
agora que now that
àmanhã de tarde tomorrow afternoon
a árvore the tree
a aula the classroom
o autor the author
bastante enough
cá here
o campo the country
a casa de campo the country house
casar(-se) to get married
chamar to call
o chão the floor, the ground
o convite the invitation
a demora the delay
o descanso the rest
descobrir to discover
a excursão the trip
o êxito the success

grande great
já não no longer
mudar-se to move
não . . . mais no longer
a obra the work
ouvir to hear; ouvir dizer que to hear
  that
parecer to seem, look; to suit; parecer-se com to resemble
o prazer the pleasure
o prelo the press; no prelo in press
a publicação the publication
o recreio the recreation, the change
sair to go out, come out, appear;
  sair de casa to go out of the house,
  leave the house
tantas vezes so often
ter notícias de to hear from
vélho -a old; o vélho the old man

EXERCISES

A. *Read.*   O amigo do autor—Ouvi dizer que o seu livro está no prelo.   Quando vai sair?

O autor—Há de sair na próxima semana.   Você quis que fizesse uma excursão consigo (*Brazilian:* com você) ao campo a semana passada.   Mas eu sabia que se não corrigisse as provas, o livro não estaria no prelo.

O amigo—Fico muito contente que não houvesse demora, porque há muita gente que pede o livro todos os dias.   Estou certo que terá grande êxito.   Agora que a obra está terminada, você pode vir à minha casa de campo passar alguns dias de descanso e de recreio.

O autor—Aceito o convite com prazer.

B. *Answer in Portuguese.* 1. Está no prelo o livro do autor?
2. Quando vai sair? 3. Porquê não foi o autor ao campo? 4.
Houve demora na publicação do livro? 5. O que vai fazer agora o
autor?

C. *Translate the English words to complete the sentence.* 1. Poderá ir para o Brasil, se *you learn* a falar o português. 2. Se o senhor
did not live em Filadélfia, *you could not go* à beira-mar tantas vezes.
3. Se eu *had had* tempo o ano passado, *I should have studied* o françês.
4. *I hear* que Maria mora no Rio. 5. Se êle *comes* àmanhã, dar-
lhe-ei o dinheiro que lhe devo. 6. O senhor pode tomar o combóio
(*Brazilian:* trem) das oito, se *it suits you.* 7. Ela *no longer* vem
aqui. 8. Eu *would not eat* tanto, se *I were not* fome. 9. *I would
give you* o meu livro, se *I had it* comigo. 10. Maria *resembles*
sua mãe.

D. *Translate.* 1. Ouvimos dizer que João se mudou para o
campo. 2. Gosta muito do campo. 3. Se lhe parecer (*or* se tiver
vontade), venha cá àmanhã de manhã. 4. Tive notícias de meu
irmão. 5. Parece-me que vai chover. 6. Ouço dizer que seu irmão
vai casar. 7. Vamo-nos mudar para a cidade. 8. O vélho caíu no
chão. 9. Saio todas as tardes depois das três. 10. Digo a João
que não caia da árvore. 11. O senhor ouviu dizer que João não
podia vir. 12. Maria acaba de sair de casa. 13. Esta obra está
no prelo, vai sair na próxima semana. 14. João parece-se com o pai.

E. *Translate.* 1. Se ninguém vier esta tarde, hei-de sair. 2. Se
dissesse a verdade, escutava-o. 3. Se soubesse que a casa era tão
vélha, mudava-se. 4. Se tiver notícias dêle, dir-lho-ei. 5. Se o
soubesse, saía imediatamente. 6. Se o senhor tivesse o dinheiro,
dava-mo? 7. Se o senhor não mo dissesse, não o acreditava. 8. Se
fizer vento, não saïremos. 9. Se não ouvisse dizer que João vinha,
não ficava. 10. Se o senhor não lesse as provas, o livro não estaria
no prelo. 11. O senhor há-de corrigir as provas, se lhe parecer.
12. Se o professor fizer a chamada, descobrirá que João não está na
aula. 13. Não morava nesta casa, se me casasse. 14. Se o não
virmos àmanhã de manhã, não esperaremos mais. 15. Não trabalho

mais, se não me pagarem.   16. Não sei se o fará.   17. Gostava de
ir ao teatro àmanhã de tarde.   18. Se eu casar, tomarei esta casa.

F. *Translate.*   1. If it rains, I shall take a streetcar and get off
in front of the church.   2. If he calls me, I shall get up and dress
very fast.   3. He heard that I did not speak (*imperfect ind.*)
Spanish.   4. I would not have moved, if I did not like the country.
5. We shall not go tomorrow morning if he does not go with us.
6. They would get married if they had enough money.   7. If she
were tired, she would go to bed.   8. I would go to sleep if I were
tired.   9. If we come early enough, he will take us with him.   10.
He did not say whether he would go with us.   11. If we had the
time, we would go to the theater with you this evening.   12. They
do not have any books.   13. He never went to church with me.
14. He would not have fallen on the ground if he had listened to me.
15. That book would not be in press if we had not read the proofs.
16. She resembles her mother.   17. I could teach you Portuguese.

Lesson XXIII

130. Verbs ending in *-iar* and *-uar*. In verbs ending in **-iar** and **-uar,** the i and the u may be looked upon as the radical vowels; they are accented in the whole singular and the third plural of the present indicative and present subjunctive. The final **e** of the first and third singular present subjunctive has the usual value of French mute *e* (of *i* in *perish* in Brazilian Portuguese).

pronunciar	*to pronounce*	continuar	*to continue*
PRES. IND.	PRES. SUBJ.	PRES. IND.	PRES. SUBJ.
pronuncio	pronuncie	continuo	continue
(pronuncias)	(pronuncies)	(continuas)	(continues)
pronuncia	pronuncie	continua	continue
pronunciamos	pronunciemos	continuamos	continuemos
(pronunciais)	(pronuncieis)	(continuais)	(continueis)
pronunciam	pronunciem	continuam	continuem

a) In some verbs ending in **-iar** and **-ear,**[1] the i and **e** change to **ei** when accented.

presenciar	*to witness, be present at*	recear	*to fear*
PRES. IND.	PRES. SUBJ.	PRES. IND.	PRES. SUBJ.
presenceio	presenceie	receio	receie
(presenceias)	(presenceies)	(receias)	(receies)
presenceia	presenceie	receia	receie
presenciamos	presenciemos	receamos	receemos
(presenciais)	(presencieis)	(receais)	(receeis)
presenceiam	presenceiem	receiam	receiem

131. Infinitive. Some verbs are followed by a dependent infinitive without a preposition, some take the preposition **a,** some take the preposition **de,** and some take other prepositions. The corresponding verbs in English are sometimes followed by the verb form in *-ing* and sometimes by the preposition *to* plus the infinitive.

---

[1] Note that the **e** of **-ear** is pronounced like the i of -iar (like English *y*) and that this similarity is true of all forms in which the stress is on the ending.

1. Verbs which take no preposition before a dependent infinitive.

contar   *to intend to, expect to*
decidir   *to decide to*
deixar   *to allow to, let*
desejar   *to desire to*
dever   *to be bound to, must*
esperar   *to hope to*
esquecer   *to forget to*
fazer   *to make*
importar   *to be important to*
ir   *to go to*
mandar   *to order to; to have, cause to*
ouvir   *to hear, hear . . . -ing*
ser   (impersonal) + adj.   *to be . . . to*
parecer   *to seem to*

pensar   *to intend to*
permitir   *to permit to*
poder   *to be able to, can*
preferir   *to prefer to*
procurar   *to try to*
proïbir   *to forbid to*
prometer   *to promise to*
querer   *to wish to, want to*
recear   *to fear to, be afraid to*
saber   *to know how to, be able to*
temer   *to fear to*
tencionar   *to intend to*
ver   *to see . . . -ing*
vir   *to come to*

Prometo estudar muito.   *I promise to study hard.*

2. Verbs which take the preposition **a** before a dependent infinitive.

aconselhar a   *to advise to*
acostumar-se a   *to accustom oneself to*
ajudar a   *to help (to)*
aprender a   *to learn (how) to*
apressar-se a   *to hurry to*
começar a   *to begin to*
continuar a   *to continue to*
convidar a (or para)   *to invite to*
decidir-se a   *to decide to*
ensinar a   *to teach (how) to*

obrigar a   *to oblige to*
pôr-se a   *to begin to*
preparar-se a (or para)   *to prepare to, get ready to*
resolver-se a   *to decide to*
subir a *to go up to*
tardar a   *to be long in . . . -ing*
tornar a   *to . . . again*
vir a   *to happen to*
voltar a   *to . . . again*

Ensinou-me a nadar.   *He taught me to swim.*

3. Verbs which take the preposition **de** before a dependent infinitive.

acabar de   *to finish . . . -ing, have just . . .*
acusar de   *to charge with . . . -ing*
cansar-se de   *to get tired of . . . -ing*
cessar de   *to cease . . . -ing*
deixar de   *to stop . . . -ing*
encarregar-se de   *to take charge of . . . -ing*

esquecer-se de   *to forget to*
folgar de   *to be glad to*
gostar de   *to like to*
lembrar-se de   *to remember to*
parar de   *to stop . . . -ing*
precisar de   *to need to*

Folgo de o ver.   *I am glad to see him.*

4. Verbs which take other prepositions before a dependent infinitive.

hesitar em	*to hesitate to*
insistir em	*to insist on . . . -ing*
acabar por	*to finish by . . . -ing*
começar por	*to begin by . . . -ing*
pedir para	*to ask to*

Insisto em fazê-lo.	*I insist on doing it.*
Começou por cantar.	*He began by singing.*
Pediu-me para lhe ajudar.	*He asked me to help him.*

132. Personal infinitive. The personal infinitive is an inflected infinitive which shows the person and number of the subject.

falar	aprender	partir	dizer
(falares)	(aprenderes)	(partires)	(dizeres)
falar	aprender	partir	dizer
falarmos	aprendermos	partirmos	dizermos
(falardes)	(aprenderdes)	(partirdes)	(dizerdes)
falarem	aprenderem	partirem	dizerem

133. Use of personal infinitive. Because it is not ambiguous as to person and number, the personal infinitive is often used instead of the indicative or the subjunctive.

Peço-lhes dinheiro por serem êles ricos.	*I ask them for money because they are rich.*
Vieram aqui sem o sabermos.	*They came here without our knowing it.*
Não é preciso estudarmos hoje.	*We do not have to study today.*

134. *Ao* + infinitive. Ao + the infinitive (personal or impersonal) is equivalent to English *on . . . -ing.*

Ao entrarmos no hotel, vimo-lo sair.	*On entering the hotel, we saw him leaving.*

VOCABULARY

acender to light
acentuar to accent
afastar-se to move away, go away
alumiar to illuminate, light up
apagar to put out, extinguish
apanhar to pick up
barbear to shave
a bôlsa the pocketbook
a calçada (*Brazilian*) sidewalk
cantar to sing
a chegada the arrival
copiar to copy
correctamente correctly
a dúvida the doubt; sem dúvida doubtless

o enderêço the address
enviar to send
excelente excellent
fechar to close, shut
jazer to lie
a lâmpada the lamp
a luz the light
o mêdo the fear; ter mêdo de to be afraid to
o mendigo the beggar
o passeio the sidewalk; *see* calçada *above*
por because of
ràpidamente quickly, rapidly
em vez de instead of

EXERCISES

A. *Read.* Estava sentado à janela do meu quarto esta manhã, quando vi um homem descer a rua. O homem era sem dúvida um mendigo. Ao chegar diante da casa, apanhou alguma coisa que jazia no passeio (*Brazilian:* na calçada). Então afastou-se ràpidamente. Mais tarde eu saí a procurá-lo, mas não tornei a vê-lo. É pena que não o pudesse achar; porque aquilo que êle apanhou na rua era a bôlsa que perdi ontem.

B. *Answer in Portuguese.* 1. Quem viu você descer a rua esta manhã? 2. Onde estava você? 3. O que fêz o mendigo quando chegou diante da casa? 4. Ficou ali muito tempo? 5. Tornou você a vê-lo? 6. O que era a coisa que apanhou o mendigo?

C. *In the following sentences, remove the dash entirely or replace it by a or de.* 1. Ajudou-me — aprender o português. 2. Convidei o amigo — jantar comigo. 3. Começámos — trabalhar muito cedo. 4. João tarda — chegar. 5. Ouvi — cantar a sua irmã ontem à noite. 6. Precisei — levantar-me antes das seis. 7. Apresse-se — acabar o seu trabalho. 8. Não me lembrei — acender a lâmpada. 9. Não nos permite — fumar. 10. Ensinou-me — falar português. 11. Procurei — fechar a porta.

D. *Translate.* 1. Como se pronuncia esta palavra? 2. Não sei como se pronuncia. 3. Quero que o senhor presenceie a chegada dos soldados. 4. Mando que os alunos copiem os exercícios. 5. A lâmpada alumia toda a aula. 6. Receio que não copiem correctamente as frases. 7. Continua o seu trabalho. 8. Envia-me cartas todas as semanas. 9. Esta palavra não se acentua. 10. Quere que os alunos pronunciem apenas dez palavras. 11. Tenho pressa; quero que me barbeie ràpidamente. 12. Sei a pronúncia destas palavras. 13. Apague a luz imediatamente.

E. *Translate.* 1. Não sei o seu enderêço e devo escrever-lhe uma carta. 2. Ajudamos os alunos a pronunciar as palavras portuguesas. 3. O professor ensina-os a falar português. 4. Canso-me de estudar todo o tempo. 5. Não me deixa apagar a lâmpada. 6. Aprendemos a falar português. 7. Devemos lembrar-nos de fechar os nossos livros. 8. Convidei-o para tomar chá comigo. 9. Meu filho gosta muito de viajar. 10. Encarrego-me de lhe ensinar o português. 11. Ouvi-o falar francês. 12. Vi João descer do automóvel. 13. Ouvimos cantar sua filha.

F. *Translate.* 1. É preciso irmos embora. 2. Ajudo-lhes a aprender o português. 3. Aconselha-nos a estudar apenas esta lição. 4. Entrou no quarto depois de eu acender a lâmpada. 5. Depois de se sentarem, tornaram a rir e a falar. 6. Nós escrevemos a carta em vez de êles a escreverem. 7. Não trabalham por serem muito ricos.

G. *Translate.* 1. They do not know how these words are pronounced. 2. I am afraid to wait here. 3. He continues to study hard. 4. We helped them to learn this lesson. 5. We taught them to pronounce difficult words. 6. They do not know how to sing. 7. I went instead of their going. 8. I sent him their address again. 9. He wants me to copy the exercises correctly. 10. We get tired of working all day. 11. We are getting ready to go to Rio. 12. She heard them arrive very late. 13. We asked them to sing. 14. He did only one exercise. 15. I always put out the light before going to bed. 16. He intended to shut the door but forgot to do it. 17. They are copying the exercises. 18. They are studying Portuguese again this year. 19. They left without coming to see me. 20. He never hesitates to tell the truth. 21. Shave me quickly; I do not wish to miss the train. 22. His pronunciation is excellent.

Lesson XXIV

135. Radical-changing nouns. Many nouns with radical close o and final o form their plural by changing the close o to open o besides the regular addition of -s.

SINGULAR	PLURAL
fọgo	fọgos
pọvo	pọvos

136. Radical-changing adjectives. Many adjectives with radical close o and final o form their masculine plural and their feminine singular and plural by changing the close o to open o besides the regular changes in ending.

MASCULINE		FEMININE	
SINGULAR	PLURAL	SINGULAR	PLURAL
nọvo	nọvos	nọva	nọvas
formọso	formọsos	formọsa	formọsas

A noteworthy exception is **todo,** which has close o in all its forms: **tọdo, tôda, tọdos, tôdas.**

137. Comparison of adjectives and adverbs. The comparative and superlative of adjectives and adverbs are formed by placing **mais** before the adjective or adverb.

POSITIVE	COMPARATIVE AND SUPERLATIVE
rico *rich*	mais rico *richer, richest*
de-vagar *slowly*	mais de-vagar *more slowly, most slowly*

Some adjectives and adverbs have irregular comparatives and superlatives.

POSITIVE	COMPARATIVE AND SUPERLATIVE
bọm *good*	melhọr *better, best*
mạu *bad*	piọr *worse, worst*
grạnde *large*	maiọr *larger, largest*
pequẹno *small*	menọr or mạis pequẹno *smaller, smallest*
bẹm *well*	melhọr *better, best*
mạl *badly, poorly*	piọr *worse, worst*
muito *much; hard*	mạis *more, most; harder*
pọuco *little*	menọs *less, least*
pọucos *few*	menọs *fewer, fewest*

112

a) The sense generally requires the use of the definite article or a possessive adjective with the superlative in English and Portuguese.

É o melhor aluno aqui.	*He is the best pupil here.*
É o aluno mais inteligente da classe.	*He is the most intelligent pupil in the class.*

b) There is an absolute superlative, formed with the ending **-íssimo,** which is not used in comparisons but which has intensive force and is equivalent to English *very* + the adjective.

É lindíssima.	*She is very pretty.*

c) The feminine of comparatives and superlatives ending in **-or** (and **-or**) is the same as the masculine.

Esta pena é a melhor.	*This pen is the best one.*

d) The preposition *in* after the superlative is translated by **de.**

É a cidade mais pequena de Portugal.	*It is the smallest city in Portugal.*

e) English *than* is translated in Portuguese by **que** or **do que** and before numerals by **de.**

Tem mais dinheiro (do) que eu.	*He has more money than I.*
Pesa mais de cem quilos.	*He weighs more than a hundred kilograms.*

f) Comparison of equality is expressed by **tão . . . como** (*Brazilian:* **quanto**) *as . . . as.*

João é tão alto como José.	*John is as tall as Joseph.*

138. Relative pronouns. 1. The most common relative pronoun is **que** *who, whom, which, that.* It is invariable, refers to persons and things, and is used as subject and object of a verb.

o senhor que mora nesta casa	*the gentleman who lives in this house*
a rapariga que vi aqui esta manhã	*the girl I saw here this morning*
o livro que está sôbre a mesa	*the book which is on the table*

2. The pronoun **quem** *who, whom* is used only of persons. It is both singular and plural.

Foi meu filho quem chegou ontem. *It was my son who arrived yesterday.*
os rapazes com quem falava *the boys with whom I was speaking*

3. **O qual** (**a qual, os quais, as quais**) may be used to avoid ambiguity.

a mãe de João, a qual está em Lisboa *John's mother, who is in Lisbon*

4. The pronoun **o que** (**a que, os que, as que**) is a combination of the relative pronoun **que** and a demonstrative pronoun antecedent. It means *he who, she who, the one who, those who, the ones who, he whom, the one which, the one that,* etc.

Êstes livros são os que desejo. *These books are the ones that I want.*
O livro que desejo é o que você *The book I want is the one you are*
está a ler. *reading.*

a) The first part, that is, the demonstrative pronoun part of these combinations, may be followed by **de** instead of the relative pronoun **que**. It then means *that of, those of.*

Êste livro e o do meu amigo *This book and that of my friend*

b) The neuter **o que** means *what, that which.*

Sabe o que disse? *Do you know what he said?*

5. The idea of antecedent and relative pronoun is combined in **quantos** (**quantas**) *all those who* (or *whom*).

Quantos o conhecem admiram-no. *All who know him admire him.*

a) The neuter **quanto** means *all that, everything that.*

Quanto diz é verdade. *Everything that he says is true.*

6. The possessive form of the relative is **cujo** (**cuja, cujos, cujas**). It agrees in gender and number with the noun it modifies.

os senhores cuja chegada espe- *the gentlemen whose arrival we are*
ramos *awaiting*

a) Other genitives are expressed by **de quem.**

o senhor de quem falei *the gentleman of whom I spoke*

VOCABULARY

algumas vezes sometimes
o almôço the lunch
alto -a tall, high
a artista the artist
o café da manhã (Brazilian) breakfast
calar-se to be silent, keep quiet
o concêrto the concert
o criado the servant, the waiter; see garçon below
os demais the rest, the others
demais too, too much
direito -a right
esquerdo -a left
a Europa Europe
a febre the fever
faz favor de please
formoso, formosa beautiful
garçon (Brazilian) waiter
interessar to interest
o jantar the dinner

o lado the side; de . . . lado on . . . side
com licença I beg your pardon
a maior parte the majority, the most
mal ill
mandar chamar to send for
a música the music
novo, nova new, recent, young
o ôlho, os olhos the eye
o ôvo, os ovos the egg
o país the country
o pequeno almôço the breakfast; see café da manhã above
perceber to understand
a pianista the pianist
o piano the piano
precisar de to need
a refeição the meal
a sala de jantar the dining room
vários -as several

EXERCISES

A. *Read.* —Com licença, senhor, faz favor de me passar o jornal, se já acabou de lê-lo.

—Aqui tem todos os jornais da manhã. Não há muito de novo. O que mais me interessou foi a chegada a êste país da famosa pianista brasileira Guiomar Novaes, que vai dar vários concertos nesta cidade antes de partir para a Europa. Gosto muito da música de piano e fico contente que tenhamos o ensejo de ouvir esta grande artista.

B. *Answer in Portuguese.* 1. O que há nos jornais da manhã? 2. Quando chegou Guiomar Novaes a êste país? 3. Quem é Guiomar Novaes? 4. Vai dar concertos nesta cidade? 5. Para onde vai depois? 6. Terão vocês o ensejo de ouvi-la?

C. *Translate the English words to complete the sentence.* 1. João é o *best* aluno *in the* classe. 2. Não percebo *what* o senhor dizia.

3. O senhor tem mais dinheiro *than* eu. 4. João é o rapaz *tallest* de todos. 5. Comprei em Paris estas luvas e *those of* Maria. 6. Portugal tem bons *harbors*. 7. Gostei muito do *breakfast* e do *lunch* que me deram. 8. José tem *fewer* livros *than* João. 9. Fala *worse than* os demais. 10. É uma rapariga (*Brazilian:* moça) muito *beautiful*. 11. Não gosto de *eggs*.

D. *Translate.* 1. Quais são os nomes das refeições em português? 2. Os nomes das refeições são o pequeno almôço (*Brazilian:* o café da manhã), o almôço, e o jantar. 3. Tomamo-las na sala de jantar. 4. Algumas vezes tomamos o pequeno almôço (*Brazilian:* o café da manhã) na cama antes de nos levantarmos. 5. Quantos almoços (*Brazilian:* cafés) querem esta manhã? 6. Somos três e queremos três almoços (*Brazilian:* cafés). 7. Tomaremos ovos. 8. Aquelas raparigas (*Brazilian:* moças) são muito formosas. 9. Esta gravata que levo é nova. 10. O novo criado fala demais; quero que se cale. 11. Portugal tem muitos e bons portos.

E. *Translate.* 1. O senhor fala de-pressa demais; fale mais de-vagar. 2. É mais vélho do que parece. 3. É o maior país da Europa. 4. Meu irmão é mais alto do que meu pai. 5. Não quero que mande chamar o médico; tenho pouca febre e estou melhor. 6. O professor tem hoje mais de vinte alunos na classe. 7. A maior parte dos novos livros são muito interessantes. 8. João é mais pobre do que eu. 9. É mais formosa do que a irmã. 10. É o pior aluno da classe. 11. Êste livro é novíssimo; acaba de sair. 12. Esta lição não é tão difícil como aquela.

F. *Translate.* 1. O senhor com quem falava é amigo de meu pai. 2. Êstes livros e os do meu amigo são muito novos. 3. É o senhor que nunca se cala. 4. Não me disse o que queria que eu fizesse. 5. Os que moram nesta cidade gostam muito dela. 6. Êle sabe quanto se acha naquêle livro. 7. Não percebe o que lê. 8. O que tem na mão é dinheiro. 9. Percebe o senhor o que lhe digo? 10. Sim, percebo. 11. De que lado da rua mora o senhor Araújo? 12. Mora do lado esquerdo; sou eu quem moro do lado direito. 13. São os livros de que preciso.

G. *Translate.*   1. Mary has beautiful eyes.   2. He drinks little wine.   3. They are taller than their father.   4. I shall send for the doctor, and I hope that you will be silent when he is here.   5. It is hard for me to believe what you tell me.   6. I do not understand what he means.   7. She lives in a new house.   8. He takes more eggs than I do for breakfast.   9. This book is better than that one. 10. This is the boy for whom I brought the new books.   11. Sometimes that waiter talks too much; I shall look for another who talks less.   12. I need the books that you gave him.   13. She lives on the left side of the avenue.   14. Mary is as beautiful as her sister. 15. I am surprised that you do not study harder.

Lesson XXV

139. Pluperfect indicative. The pluperfect indicative is formed by dropping the last syllable, **-ram,** of the third plural preterit indicative and adding **-ra, -ras, -ra, -ramos, -reis, -ram.** The vowel preceding **-ramos** and **-reis** takes a written accent. This accent is acute in all verbs except regular verbs of the second conjugation and **ser** (and **ir**), where it is circumflex.

Inf.	falar	aprender	partir	dizer	ser and ir
3d pl. pret. ind.	fala-ram	aprende-ram	parti-ram	disse-ram	fo-ram
Pluperf. ind.	fala-ra	aprende-ra	parti-ra	disse-ra	fo-ra
	(fala-ras)	(aprende-ras)	(parti-ras)	(disse-ras)	(fo-ras)
	fala-ra	aprende-ra	parti-ra	disse-ra	fo-ra
	falá-ramos	aprendê-ramos	partí-ramos	dissé-ramos	fô-ramos
	(falá-reis)	(aprendê-reis)	(partí-reis)	(dissé-reis)	(fô-reis)
	fala-ram	aprende-ram	parti-ram	disse-ram	fo-ram

140. Past participle. The past participle is formed by dropping the ending of the infinitive and adding **-ado** to verbs of the first conjugation and **-ido** to all other verbs.

Inf.	fal-ar	aprend-er	part-ir
Past part.	fal-ado	aprend-ido	part-ido

1. Some verbs have irregular past participles.

abrir: aberto *opened*
cobrir: coberto *covered*
descobrir: descoberto *discovered*
dizer: dito *told*
escrever: escrito *written*

morrer: *to die*: morto *died*
fazer: feito *made, done*
pôr: pôsto *put, placed*
vir: vindo *come*
ver: visto *seen*

2. Some verbs of the first conjugation have shortened past participles.

aceitar: aceito *accepted*
entregar: entregue *delivered*

gastar: gasto *spent*
ganhar: ganho [1] *earned*
pagar: pago *paid*

[1] The accented radical **a** of this verb is open in spite of the following **nh.**

118

141. Compound past tenses.   1. The perfect indicative is formed with the present indicative of **ter** and the past participle.

tenho falado	temos falado
(tens falado)	(tendes falado)
tem falado	têm and teem falado

2. The perfect subjunctive is formed with the present subjunctive of **ter** and the past participle.

tenha falado	tenhamos falado
(tenhas falado)	(tenhais falado)
tenha falado	tenham falado

3. The compound pluperfect indicative is formed with the imperfect indicative of **ter** or **haver** and the past participle.

tinha falado	havia falado
(tinhas falado)	(havias falado)
tinha falado	havia falado
tínhamos falado	havíamos falado
(tínheis falado)	(havíeis falado)
tinham falado	haviam falado

4. The pluperfect subjunctive is formed with the imperfect subjunctive of **ter** or **haver** and the past participle.

tivesse falado	houvesse falado
(tivesses falado)	(houvesses falado)
tivesse falado	houvesse falado
tivéssemos falado	houvéssemos falado
(tivésseis falado)	(houvésseis falado)
tivessem falado	houvessem falado

142. Use of perfect indicative.   The perfect indicative is used much less in Portuguese than in other Romance languages.   While the preterit indicative expresses a simple action or state in the recent or the remote past (section 84) and the imperfect indicative a continuing, repeated, or habitual action or state in a completely elapsed past (section 101), the perfect indicative expresses a continuing or repeated action or state in a past that is felt to be somewhat merged into the present.   The nearest English equivalent is perhaps the perfect progressive.

Êle tem-me escrito.	*He has been writing to me.*
Tenho estado em Lisboa.	*I have been staying in Lisbon.*

143. Use of pluperfect indicatives.   The time of the pluperfect is past from the point of view of the past.   The simple pluperfect (section 139) is used less frequently in Portuguese than the compound pluperfects (section 141) particularly in the third person plural, where either of the compound forms is always preferred because the simple form is identical with the third plural of the preterit indicative.

Não aprendera o português.	*He had not learned Portuguese.*
Não tinham aprendido o português.	*They had not learned Portuguese.*

144. The imperfect of *acabar de*.   As the present tense of **acabar de** has the force of a past tense (section 72), the imperfect has the force of a pluperfect tense.

Acabava de chegar.	*He had just arrived.*

145. Passive voice.   The passive voice is formed with the verb **ser** and the past participle, which agrees in gender and number with the subject.

Aquêle livro foi escrito por Eça de Queiroz.	*That book was written by Eça de Queiroz.*

146. Definite article (continued).   The forms of the definite article combine with the preposition **por** as follows.

por + o:	pelo	por + os:	pelos
por + a:	pela	por + as:	pelas

147. The diminutive *-inho*.   The diminutive **-inho -a** is widely used in Portuguese, with values that are hard to define.

lição *lesson*
cedo *early*
de-vagar *slow, slowly*
só *alone*
culpado *guilty, to blame*
bocado *piece, bit*

liçãozinha *little bit of a lesson*
cedinho *pretty early*
de-vagarinho *slow and easy*
sòzinho *all alone*
culpadinho *somewhat to blame*
bocadinho *little bit; little while*

VOCABULARY

os Açôres the Azores
   aí por about
a algibeira the pocket
a América America
o andar the floor; o primeiro andar the
   second floor
o avião the airplane
a carne the meat
   caro (*adv.*) dear
   chegar a to amount to; chegar para
   to be enough to *or* for
   Colombo Columbus
   consertar to mend, repair
a criada the maid
   custar to cost
a descoberta the discovery
o descobridor the discoverer
o empregado the clerk, the salesman
   famoso, famosa famous

a farmácia the drugstore
o grupo the group
a ilha the island
   levar to take (*of time*)
   mandar to have, cause
o mar the sea
   não é (assim)? is it not so?
o Oceano Atlântico the Atlantic Ocean
   pertencer to belong
o português the Portuguese
o prédio the building, the property
   quanto tempo? how long?
o rés-do-chão the ground floor, the
   first floor
   só only
   sòmente only
a travessia the crossing
   tudo everything, all
   ùltimamente lately

EXERCISES

A. *Read.* Os Açôres são um grupo de nove ilhas no Oceano
Atlântico que pertencem a Portugal. Foram descobertas pelos
portugueses aí pelo ano de mil quatrocentos-e-trinta-e-um, mais de
sessenta anos antes da descoberta da América por Colombo. A
cidade da Horta na ilha do Fayal é conhecida hoje por ser um pôrto
importante dos famosos aviões "Clipper," que levam sòmente vinte-
e-duas horas para fazer a travessia de Nova York a Lisboa.

B. *Answer in Portuguese.* 1. O que são os Açôres? 2. Quem
os descobriu? 3. Em que ano foram descobertos? 4. O que é a

Horta?   5. Quanto tempo levam os aviões para fazer a travessia do mar?

C. *Translate the English words to complete the sentence.*   1. Maria *has been studying* o português.   2. José *had left* quando eu cheguei.   3. A carta *was written* pelo amigo do professor.   4. A conta *was paid* pela criada.   5. João *had just* comer.   6. Êles *have lived* comigo muito tempo mas partiram para a Europa a semana passada.   7. Nós *have told him* a verdade muitas vezes mas não nos tem acreditado.   8. Elas *had arrived* cedo.   9. Fico contente que José *has been studying*.

D. *Translate.*   1. O senhor tem morado em Nova York, não é assim?   2. Sim, senhor, tenho morado em Nova York e meu irmão tem morado comigo.   3. O meu quarto tem sido no primeiro andar e devo subir ao segundo andar para tomar um banho.   4. Êle tinha consertado o automóvel?   5. Sim, tinha-o consertado e pudemos partir às sete da manhã.   6. Aquêle rapaz tem gasto muito dinheiro ùltimamente.   7. Tínhamos aprendido (*or* aprendêramos) muito naquela classe.   8. A carta foi escrita por um senhor que você não conhece.   9. Êste livro é vendido na loja de-fronte; vendem-no ali.   10. Êste livro está vendido, você não pode comprá-lo.   11. Déramos (*or* tínhamos dado) um passeio no jardim antes das seis.   12. As janelas foram fechadas pelos criados.   13. Haviam saído quando chegámos.   14. Tudo foi perdido.

E. *Translate.*   1. A farmácia é no rés-do-chão.   2. O chá que temos não chega para tôda essa gente.   3. Só chega para cinco pessoas.   4. Levantaram-se cedinho.   5. Essa rapariga fala devagarinho.   6. É um prédio de cinco andares.   7. Vou mandar consertar os meus sapatos.   8. O alfaiate consertou o meu fato (*Brazilian:* terno).   9. Tenho que descer ao rés-do-chão para tomar o pequeno almôço (*Brazilian:* o café da manhã).   10. Pedi ao empregado para me mostrar as gravatas.   11. Comprei algumas.   12. A conta chegou a dois dólares.   13. Tudo naquela loja custa muito caro.   14. As farmácias norte-americanas vendem tudo.   15. Deram-me um bocadinho de carne.   16. Espere aqui um bocadinho.

F. *Translate.* 1. The doors were opened by the maid. 2. They had paid the bill when I came down. 3. You had your shoes mended, did you not? 4. Yes, I had my shoes mended and my suit repaired. 5. We have been working in New York. 6. That building has four floors. 7. The weather has been bad lately. 8. The money I had in my pocket was not enough to pay the bill. 9. I had told him not to come. 10. You must get up pretty early if you wish to go with us. 11. Did you buy any books today? 12. Yes, I bought some; I have been buying books every day. 13. I studied a little bit this morning.

Appendix

148. Conjugations of regular verbs.

IMPERSONAL INFINITIVE

falạr *to speak*   **aprendẹr** *to learn*   **partịr** *to leave*

PERSONAL INFINITIVE

falạr	aprendẹr	partịr
(falạres)	(aprendẹres)	(partịres)
falạr	aprendẹr	partịr
falạrmos	aprendẹrmos	partịrmos
(falạrdes)	(aprendẹrdes)	(partịrdes)
falạrem	aprendẹrem	partịrem

GERUND

falạndo *speaking*   **aprendẹndo** *learning*   **partịndo** *leaving*

PAST PARTICIPLE

falạdo	aprendịdo	partịdo

INDICATIVE

PRESENT

fạlo	aprẹndo	pạrto
(fạlas)	(aprẹndes)	(pạrtes)
fạla	aprẹnde	pạrte
falạmos	aprendẹmos	partịmos
(falạis)	(aprendẹis)	(partịs)
fạlam	aprẹndem	(pạrtem

IMPERFECT

falạva	aprendịa	partịa
(falạvas)	(aprendịas)	(partịas)
falạva	aprendịa	partịa
falávamos	aprendíamos	partíamos
(faláveis)	(aprendíeis)	(partíeis)
falạvam	aprendịam	partịam

125

PRETERIT

falęi	aprendį	partį
(faląste)	(aprendęste)	(partįste)
falọu	aprendęu	partįu
falámos	aprendęmos	partįmos
(faląstes)	(aprendęstes)	(partįstes)
faląram	aprendęram	partįram

PLUPERFECT

faląra	aprendęra	partįra
(faląras)	(aprendęras)	(partįras)
faląra	aprendęra	partįra
faláramos	aprendêramos	partíramos
(faláreis)	(aprendêreis)	(partíreis)
faląram	aprendęram	partįram

FUTURE

falaręi	aprenderęi	partiręi
(falarás)	(aprenderás)	(partirás)
falará	aprenderá	partirá
falaręmos	aprenderęmos	partiręmos
(falaręis)	(aprenderęis)	(partiręis)
falarão	aprenderão	partirão

CONDITIONAL

falarįa	aprenderįa	partirįa
(falarįas)	(aprenderįas)	(partirįas)
falarįa	aprenderįa	partirįa
falaríamos	aprenderíamos	partiríamos
(falaríeis)	(aprenderíeis)	(partiríeis)
falarįam	aprenderįam	partirįam

IMPERATIVE [1]

2d sg.	(fąla)	(apręnde)	(pąrte)
2d pl.	(faląi)	(aprendęi)	(partį)

[1] The imperative forms are used only in affirmative commands in speech in which the pronouns **tu** and **vós** would be used (see section 58 and section 78 a). They are replaced by the third person forms of the present subjunctive (see section 87 and note 1 on page 84).

In negative commands in speech in which **tu** and **vós** would be used, the imperative forms are replaced by the second singular and plural of the present subjunctive.

SUBJUNCTIVE

PRESENT

fale	aprenda	parta
(fales)	(aprendas)	(partas)
fale	aprenda	parta
falemos	aprendamos	partamos
(faleis)	(aprendais)	(partais)
falem	aprendam	partam

IMPERFECT

falasse	aprendesse	partisse
(falasses)	(aprendesses)	(partisses)
falasse	aprendesse	partisse
falássemos	aprendêssemos	partíssemos
(falásseis)	(aprendêsseis)	(partísseis)
falassem	aprendessem	partissem

FUTURE

falar	aprender	partir
(falares)	(aprenderes)	(partires)
falar	aprender	partir
falarmos	aprendermos	partirmos
(falardes)	(aprenderdes)	(partirdes)
falarem	aprenderem	partirem

149. Orthographic–changing verbs.   Verbs in -car.

ficar   *to stay, remain*

PRETERIT IND.	PRES. SUBJ.
fiquei	fique
(ficaste)	(fiques)
ficou	fique
ficámos	fiquemos
(ficastes)	(fiqueis)
ficaram	fiquem

150. Orthographic-changing verbs. Verbs in -gar.

chegar   *to arrive*

PRETERIT IND.	PRES. SUBJ.
cheguei	chegue
(chegaste)	(chegues)
chegou	chegue
chegámos	cheguemos
(chegastes)	(chegueis)
chegaram	cheguem

151. Orthographic-changing verbs. Verbs in -ger and -gir.

corrigir   *to correct*

PRES. IND.	PRES SUBJ.
corrijo	corrija
(corriges)	(corrijas)
corrige	corrija
corrigimos	corrijamos
(corrigis)	(corrijais)
corrigem	corrijam

152. Orthographic-changing verbs. Verbs in -guir.

seguir   *to follow*

PRES. IND.	PRES. SUBJ.
sigo	siga
(segues)	(sigas)
segue	siga
seguimos	sigamos
(seguis)	(sigais)
seguem	sigam

153. Orthographic-changing verbs. Verbs in -çar.

começar   *to begin*

PRETERIT IND.	PRES. SUBJ.
comecei	comece
(começaste)	(comeces)
começou	comece
começámos	comecemos
(começastes)	(comeceis)
começaram	comecem

154. Orthographic-changing verbs.   Verbs in -cer and -cir.

esquecer   *to forget*

PRES IND.	PRES. SUBJ.
esqueço	esqueça
(esqueces)	(esqueças)
esquece	esqueça
esquecemos [1]	esqueçamos [1]
(esqueceis)	(esqueçais)
esquecem	esqueçam

155. Radical-changing verbs.   Verbs with radical e.

1. **levar** *to take away*   2. **dever** *to owe, to have to*   3. **servir** *to serve*

PRES. IND.

levo	devo	sirvo
(levas)	(deves)	(serves)
leva	deve	serve
levamos	devemos	servimos
(levais)	(deveis)	(servis)
levam	devem	servem

PRES. SUBJ.

leve	deva	sirva
(leves)	(devas)	(sirvas)
leve	deva	sirva
levemos	devamos	sirvamos
(leveis)	(devais)	(sirvais)
levem	devam	sirvam

4. Radical **e**, followed by **m** or **n** in the same syllable, accented or unaccented, is always close (sections 3, 2 a and 8, 2), except in the first singular present indicative and the whole present subjunctive of verbs of the third conjugation, where it is changed to **i**. Therefore, of the following three verbs, only **sentir** is radical-changing.

[1] See note 3, p. 93.

sentar *to seat*	**vender** *to sell*	**sentir** *to feel*
	PRES. IND.	
sẹnto	vẹndo	sịnto
(sẹntas)	(vẹndes)	(sẹntes)
sẹnta	vẹnde	sẹnte
sentạmos	vendẹmos	sentịmos
(sentạis)	(vendẹis)	(sentịs)
sẹntam	vẹndem	sẹntem
	PRES. SUBJ.	
sẹnte	vẹnda	sịnta
(sẹntes)	(vẹndas)	(sịntas)
sẹnte	vẹnda	sịnta
sentẹmos	vendạmos	sintạmos
(sentẹis)	(vendạis)	(sintạis)
sẹntem	vẹndam	sịntam

5. Radical **e**, followed by soft **g, j, lh, nh, ch, x,** or **s** (Eng. *sh* in *shall*), is pronounced like English *i* in *perish*, when unaccented, e.g., **aconselhar, desejar, mexer, vestir.**

156. Radical-changing verbs. Verbs with radical *o*.

1. **tomar** *to get*	2. **mover** *to move*	3. **dormir** *to sleep*
	PRES. IND.	
tọmo	mọvo	dụrmo
(tọmas)	(mọves)	(dọrmes)
tọma	mọve	dọrme
tomạmos	movẹmos	dormịmos
(tomạis)	(movẹis)	(dormịs)
tọmam	mọvem	dọrmem
	PRES. SUBJ.	
tọme	mọva	dụrma
(tọmes)	(mọvas)	(dụrmas)
tọme	mọva	dụrma
tomẹmos	movạmos	durmạmos
(tomẹis)	(movạis)	(durmạis)
tọmem	mọvam	dụrmam

4. Radical **o**, followed by **m** or **n** in the same syllable, accented or unaccented, is always close (sections 5, 2 a and 10, 2).   There-

fore, such verbs as **contar** *to count* and **romper** *to break* are not radical-changing verbs.

5. The **o** of **voltar** and **folgar** is open in the accented forms and close in the unaccented forms, e.g., vǫlto, vǫltamos.

6. Radical **o** in verbs in **-oar** is close when accented and pronounced like English *w* when unaccented. The **e** of the endings of the whole singular present subjunctive is pronounced like French mute *e* (like *i* in *perish* in Brazilian Portuguese) as in regular verbs.

perdoạr *to pardon*

PRES. IND.	PRES. SUBJ.
perdǫo	perdǫe
(perdǫas)	(perdǫes)
perdǫa	perdǫe
perdoạmos (w)	perdoẹmos (w)
(perdoạis) (w)	(perdoẹis) (w)
perdǫam	perdǫem

7. Radical **o** in verbs in **-oer** has the usual changes of radical-changing verbs. The **e** of the endings of the second and third singular present indicative is pronounced like English *y* and has been changed in spelling to *i*.

doẹr *to pain, ache*

PRES. IND.	PRES. SUBJ.
dǫo	dǫa
(dóis)	(dǫas)
dói	dǫa
doẹmos	doạmos
(doẹis)	(doạis)
dǫem	dǫam

157. Radical-changing verbs. Verbs of the third conjugation with radical *u*.

1. **subịr** *to go up, come up*

PRES. IND.	PRES. SUBJ.
sụbo	sụba
(sǫbes)	(sụbas)
sǫbe	sụba
subịmos	subạmos
(subịs)	(subạis)
sǫbem	sụbam

2. Two verbs in **-uir, construir** and **destruir,** may be conjugated like **subir** or may keep the **u** in all forms.   In either case the **e** of the endings of the second and third singular present indicative is pronounced like English **y** and has been changed in spelling to **i.**

construir   *to construct*

PRES. IND.	PRES. SUBJ.
construo	construa
(construóis) or (construis)	(construas)
construói or construi	construa
construímos	construamos
(construís)	(construais)
construem or construem	construam

158. Verbs in *-iar, -ear,* and *-uar.*   1. The **i** of **-iar** and the **e** of **-ear** are treated as radical vowels.   When accented they change to **ei,** and when unaccented they are pronounced like English **y.**

recear   *to fear*

PRES. IND.	PRES. SUBJ.
receio	receie
(receias)	(receies)
receia	receie
receamos	receemos
(receais)	(receeis)
receiam	receiem

2. In some verbs in **-iar** the **i** remains unchanged when accented.

pronunciar   *to pronounce*

PRES. IND.	PRES. SUBJ.
pronuncio	pronuncie
(pronuncias)	(pronuncies)
pronuncia	pronuncie
pronunciamos	pronunciemos
(pronunciais)	(pronuncieis)
pronunciam	pronunciem

3. The **u** of **-uar** is treated as a radical vowel and is, therefore, accented in the whole singular and the third plural present indicative and present subjunctive.

continuar *to continue*

PRES. IND.	PRES. SUBJ.
continuo	continue
(continuas)	(continues)
continua	continue
continuamos	continuemos
(continuais)	(continueis)
continuam	continuem

134 APPENDIX

INFINITIVE IMPERSONAL & PERSONAL	GERUND AND PAST PARTICIPLE	PRESENT INDICATIVE	PRESENT SUBJUNCTIVE	IMPERFECT INDICATIVE	FUTURE INDICATIVE
159. cabẹr *to fit*					
cabẹr	cabẹndo	cạibo	cạiba	cabịa	caberẹi
(cabẹres)		(cạbes)	(cạibas)	(cabịas)	(caberás)
cabẹr		cạbe	cạiba	cabịa	caberá
cabẹrmos	cabịdo	cabẹmos	caibạmos	cabíamos	caberẹmos
(cabẹrdes)		(cabẹis)	(caibạis)	(cabíeis)	(caberẹis)
cabẹrem		cạbem	cạibam	cabịam	caberão
160. caịr *to fall*					
caịr	caịndo	cạio	cạia	caía	caïrẹi
(caíres)		(cạis)	(cạias)	(caías)	(caïrás)
caịr		cại	cạia	caía	caïrá
caírmos	caído	caímos	caiạmos	caíamos	caïrẹmos
(caírdes)		(caís)	(caiạis)	(caíeis)	(caïrẹis)
caírem		cạem	cạiam	caíam	caïrão
161. crẹr *to believe*					
crẹr	crẹndo	crẹio	crẹia	crịa	crerẹi
(crẹres)		(crês)	(crẹias)	(crịas)	(crerás)
crẹr		crê	crẹia	crịa	crerá
crẹrmos	crịdo	crẹmos	creạmos	críamos	crerẹmos
(crẹrdes)		(crẹdes)	(creạis)	(críeis)	(crerẹis)
crẹrem		crêem	crẹiam	crịam	crerão
162. dạr *to give*					
dạr	dạndo	dọu	dê	dạva	darẹi
(dạres)		(dás)	(dês)	(dạvas)	(darás)
dạr		dá	dê	dạva	dará
dạrmos	dạdo	dạmos	dêmos	dávamos	darẹmos
(dạrdes)		(dạis)	(dẹis)	(dáveis)	(darẹis)
dạrem		dão	dêem	dạvam	darão

IRREGULAR VERBS

135

CONDITIONAL	PRETERIT INDICATIVE	PLUPERFECT INDICATIVE	IMPERFECT SUBJUNCTIVE	FUTURE SUBJUNCTIVE	IMPERATIVE
caberia	coube	coubera	coubesse	couber	
(caberias)	(coubeste)	(couberas)	(coubesses)	(couberes)	(cabe)
caberia	coube	coubera	coubesse	couber	
caberíamos	coubemos	coubéramos	coubéssemos	coubermos	
(caberíeis)	(coubestes)	(coubéreis)	(coubésseis)	(couberdes)	(cabei)
caberiam	couberam	couberam	coubessem	couberem	
caïria	caí	caíra	caísse	cair	
(caïrias)	(caíste)	(caíras)	(caísses)	(caíres)	(cai)
caïria	caíu	caíra	caísse	cair	
caïríamos	caímos	caíramos	caíssemos	caírmos	
(caïríeis)	(caístes)	(caíreis)	(caísseis)	(caírdes)	(caí)
caïriam	caíram	caíram	caíssem	caírem	
creria	crí	crera	cresse	crer	
(crerias)	(crêste)	(creras)	(cresses)	(creres)	(crê)
creria	creu	crera	cresse	crer	
creríamos	cremos	crêramos	crêssemos	crermos	
(creríeis)	(crêstes)	(crêreis)	(crêsseis)	(crerdes)	(crede)
creriam	creram	creram	cressem	crerem	
daria	dei	dera	desse	der	
(darias)	(deste)	(deras)	(desses)	(deres)	(dá)
daria	deu	dera	desse	der	
daríamos	demos	déramos	déssemos	dermos	
(daríeis)	(destes)	(déreis)	(désseis)	(derdes)	(dai)
dariam	deram	deram	dessem	derem	

INFINITIVE IMPERSONAL & PERSONAL	GERUND AND PAST PARTICIPLE	PRESENT INDICATIVE	PRESENT SUBJUNCTIVE	IMPERFECT INDICATIVE	FUTURE INDICATIVE
163. dizẹr *to say, tell*					
dizẹr	dizẹndo	dịgo	dịga	dizịa	dirẹi
(dizẹres)		(dịzes)	(dịgas)	(dizịas)	(dirás)
dizẹr	dịto	dịz	dịga	dizịa	dirá
dizẹrmos		dizẹmos	digạmos	dizíamos	dirẹmos
(dizẹrdes)		(dizẹis)	(digạis)	(dizíeis)	(dirẹis)
dizẹrem		dịzem	dịgam	dizịam	dirão
164. estạr *to be*					
estạr	estạndo	estọu	estẹja	estạva	estarẹi
(estạres)		(estás)	(estẹjas)	(estạvas)	(estarás)
estạr	estạdo	está	estẹja	estạva	estará
estạrmos		estạmos	estejạmos	estávamos	estarẹmos
(estạrdes)		(estạis)	(estejạis)	(estáveis)	(estarẹis)
estạrem		estão	estẹjam	estạvam	estarão
165. fazẹr *to do*					
fazẹr	fazẹndo	fạço	fạça	fazịa	farẹi
(fazẹres)		(fạzes)	(fạças)	(fazịas)	(farás)
fazẹr	fẹito	fạz	fạça	fazịa	fará
fazẹrmos		fazẹmos	façạmos	fazíamos	farẹmos
(fazẹrdes)		(fazẹis)	(façạis)	(fazíeis)	(farẹis)
fazẹrem		fạzem	fạçam	fazịam	farão
166. havẹr *to have*					
havẹr	havẹndo	hẹi	hạja	havịa	haverẹi
(havẹres)		(hás)	(hạjas)	(havịas)	(haverás)
havẹr	havịdo	há	hạja	havịa	haverá
havẹrmos		havẹmos	hajạmos	havíamos	haverẹmos
(havẹrdes)		(havẹis)	(hajạis)	(havíeis)	(haverẹis)
havẹrem		hão	hạjam	havịam	haverão

CONDITIONAL	PRETERIT INDICATIVE	PLUPERFECT INDICATIVE	IMPERFECT SUBJUNCTIVE	FUTURE SUBJUNCTIVE	IMPERATIVE
diria	disse	dissęra	dissęsse	dissęr	
(dirias)	(dissęste)	(dissęras)	(dissęsses)	(dissęres)	(diz) (dize)
diria	disse	dissęra	dissęsse	dissęr	
diríamos	dissęmos	disséramos	disséssemos	dissęrmos	
(diríeis)	(dissęstes)	(disséreis)	(dissésseis)	(dissęrdes)	(dizęi)
diriam	dissęram	dissęram	dissęssem	dissęrem	
estaria	estive	estivęra	estivęsse	estivęr	
(estarias)	(estivęste)	(estivęras)	(estivęsses)	(estivęres)	(está)
estaria	estęve	estivęra	estivęsse	estivęr	
estaríamos	estivęmos	estivéramos	estivéssemos	estivęrmos	
(estaríeis)	(estivęstes)	(estivéreis)	(estivésseis)	(estivęrdes)	(estai)
estariam	estivęram	estivęram	estivęssem	estivęrem	
faria	fiz	fizęra	fizęsse	fizęr	
(farias)	(fizęste)	(fizęras)	(fizęsses)	(fizęres)	(faz) (faze)
faria	fêz	fizęra	fizęsse	fizęr	
faríamos	fizęmos	fizéramos	fizéssemos	fizęrmos	
(faríeis)	(fizęstes)	(fizéreis)	(fizésseis)	(fizęrdes)	(fazęi)
fariam	fizęram	fizęram	fizęssem	fizęrem	
haveria	houve	houvęra	houvęsse	houvęr	
(haverias)	(houvęste)	(houvęras)	(houvęsses)	(houvęres)	(há)
haveria	houve	houvęra	houvęsse	houvęr	
haveríamos	houvęmos	houvéramos	houvéssemos	houvęrmos	
(haveríeis)	(houvęstes)	(houvéreis)	(houvésseis)	(houvęrdes)	(havęi)
haveriam	houvęram	houvęram	houvęssem	houvęrem	

INFINITIVE IMPERSONAL & PERSONAL	GERUND AND PAST PARTICIPLE	PRESENT INDICATIVE	PRESENT SUBJUNCTIVE	IMPERFECT INDICATIVE	FUTURE INDICATIVE
167. ịr *to go*					
ịr	ịndo	vọu	vá	ịa	irẹi
(ịres)		(vạis)	(vás)	(ịas)	(irás)
ịr	ịdo	vại	vá	ịa	irá
ịrmos		vạmos	vạmos	íamos	irẹmos
(ịrdes)		(ịdes)	(vạdes)	(íeis)	(irẹis)
ịrem		vão	vão	ịam	irão
168. jazẹr [1] *to lie*					
jazẹr	jazẹndo	jạço	jạça	jazịa	jazerẹi
(jazẹres)		(jạzes)	(jạças)	(jazịas)	(jazerás)
jazẹr	jazịdo	jạz	jạça	jazịa	jazerá
jazẹrmos		jazẹmos	jaçạmos	jazíamos	jazerẹmos
(jazẹrdes)		(jazẹis)	(jaçạis)	(jazíeis)	(jazerẹis)
jazẹrem		jạzem	jạçam	jazịam	jazerão
169. lẹr *to read*					
lẹr	lẹndo	lẹio	lẹia	lịa	lerẹi
(lẹres)		(lês)	(lẹias)	(lịas)	(lerás)
lẹr	lịdo	lê	lẹia	lịa	lerá
lẹrmos		lêmos	leạmos	líamos	lerẹmos
(lẹrdes)		(lẹdes)	(leạis)	(líeis)	(lerẹis)
lẹrem		lêem	lẹiam	lịam	lerão
170. medịr *to measure*					
medịr	medịndo	mẹço	mẹça	medịa	medirẹi
(medịres)		(mẹdes)	(mẹças)	(medịas)	(medirás)
medịr		mẹde	mẹça	medịa	medirá
medịrmos	medịdo	medịmos	meçạmos	medíamos	medirẹmos
(medịrdes)		(medịs)	(meçạis)	(medíeis)	(medirẹis)
medịrem		mẹdem	mẹçam	medịam	medirão

[1] This verb is also conjugated regularly except for the third singular present indicative, which is always **jaz**.

CONDITIONAL	PRETERIT INDICATIVE	PLUPERFECT INDICATIVE	IMPERFECT SUBJUNCTIVE	FUTURE SUBJUNCTIVE	IMPERATIVE
iria	fui	fôra	fosse	for	
(irias)	(foste)	(fôras)	(fosses)	(fores)	(vai)
iria	foi	fôra	fosse	for	
iríamos	fomos	fôramos	fôssemos	formos	
(iríeis)	(fostes)	(fôreis)	(fôsseis)	(fordes)	(ide)
iriam	foram	foram	fossem	forem	
jazeria	jouve	jouvera	jouvesse	jouver	
(jazerias)	(jouveste)	(jouveras)	(jouvesses)	(jouveres)	(jaz) (jaze)
jazeria	jouve	jouvera	jouvesse	jouver	
jazeríamos	jouvemos	jouvéramos	jouvéssemos	jouvermos	
(jazeríeis)	(jouvestes)	(jouvéreis)	(jouvésseis)	(jouverdes)	(jazei)
jazeriam	jouveram	jouveram	jouvessem	jouverem	
leria	li	lera	lesse	ler	
(lerias)	(lêste)	(leras)	(lesses)	(leres)	(lê)
leria	leu	lera	lesse	ler	
leríamos	lêmos	lêramos	lêssemos	lermos	
(leríeis)	(lêstes)	(lêreis)	(lêsseis)	(lerdes)	(lede)
leriam	leram	leram	lessem	lerem	
mediria	medi	medira	medisse	medir	
(medirias)	(mediste)	(mediras)	(medisses)	(medires)	(mede)
mediria	mediu	medira	medisse	medir	
mediríamos	medimos	medíramos	medíssemos	medirmos	
(mediríeis)	(medistes)	(medíreis)	(medísseis)	(medirdes)	(medi)
mediriam	mediram	mediram	medissem	medirem	

INFINITIVE IMPERSONAL & PERSONAL	GERUND AND PAST PARTICIPLE	PRESENT INDICATIVE	PRESENT SUBJUNCTIVE	IMPERFECT INDICATIVE	FUTURE INDICATIVE
171. ouvịr *to hear*					
ouvịr	ouvịndo	ọuço and ọiço	ọuça and ọiça	ouvịa	ouvirẹi
(ouvịres)		(ọuves)	(ọuças)	(ouvịas)	(ouvirás)
ouvịr		ọuve	ọuça	ouvịa	ouvirá
ouvịrmos	ouvịdo	ouvịmos	ouçạmos	ouvíamos	ouvirẹmos
(ouvịrdes)		(ouvịs)	(ouçạis)	(ouvíeis)	(ouvirẹis)
ouvịrem		ọuvem	ọuçam	ouvịam	ouvirão
172. pedịr *to ask*					
pedịr	pedịndo	pẹço	pẹça	pedịa	pedirẹi
(pedịres)		(pẹdes)	(pẹças)	(pedịas)	(pedirás)
pedịr		pẹde	pẹça	pedịa	pedirá
pedịrmos	pedịdo	pedịmos	peçạmos	pedíamos	pedirẹmos
(pedịrdes)		(pedịs)	(peçạis)	(pedíeis)	(pedirẹis)
pedịrem		pẹdem	pẹçam	pedịam	pedirão
173. perdẹr *to lose*					
perdẹr	perdẹndo	pẹrco	pẹrca	perdịa	perderẹi
(perdẹres)		(pẹrdes)	(pẹrcas)	(perdịas)	(perderás)
perdẹr		pẹrde	pẹrca	perdịa	perderá
perdẹrmos	perdịdo	perdẹmos	percạmos	perdíamos	perderẹmos
(perdẹrdes)		(perdẹis)	(percạis)	(perdíeis)	(perderẹis)
perdẹrem		pẹrdem	pẹrcam	perdịam	perderão
174. podẹr *to be able*					
podẹr	podẹndo	pọsso	pọssa	podịa	poderẹi
(podẹres)		(pọdes)	(pọssas)	(podịas)	(poderás)
podẹr		pọde	pọssa	podịa	poderá
podẹrmos	podịdo	podẹmos	possạmos	podíamos	poderẹmos
(podẹrdes)		(podẹis)	(possạis)	(podíeis)	(poderẹis)
podẹrem		pọdem	pọssam	podịam	poderão

CONDITIONAL	PRETERIT INDICATIVE	PLUPERFECT INDICATIVE	IMPERFECT SUBJUNCTIVE	FUTURE SUBJUNCTIVE	IMPERATIVE
ouviria	ouvi	ouvira	ouvisse	ouvir	
(ouvirias)	(ouviste)	(ouviras)	(ouvisses)	(ouvires)	(ouve)
ouviria	ouviu	ouvira	ouvisse	ouvir	
ouviríamos	ouvimos	ouvíramos	ouvíssemos	ouvirmos	
(ouviríeis)	(ouvistes)	(ouvíreis)	(ouvísseis)	(ouvirdes)	(ouvi)
ouviriam	ouviram	ouviram	ouvissem	ouvirem	
pediria	pedi	pedira	pedisse	pedir	
(pedirias)	(pediste)	(pediras)	(pedisses)	(pedires)	(pede)
pediria	pediu	pedira	pedisse	pedir	
pediríamos	pedimos	pedíramos	pedíssemos	pedirmos	
(pediríeis)	(pedistes)	(pedíreis)	(pedísseis)	(pedirdes)	(pedi)
pediriam	pediram	pediram	pedissem	pedirem	
perderia	perdi	perdera	perdesse	perder	
(perderias)	(perdeste)	(perderas)	(perdesses)	(perderes)	(perde)
perderia	perdeu	perdera	perdesse	perder	
perderíamos	perdemos	perdêramos	perdêssemos	perdermos	
(perderíeis)	(perdestes)	(perdêreis)	(perdêsseis)	(perderdes)	(perdei)
perderiam	perderam	perderam	perdessem	perderem	
poderia	pude	pudera	pudesse	puder	
(poderias)	(pudeste)	(puderas)	(pudesses)	(puderes)	(pode)
poderia	pôde	pudera	pudesse	puder	
poderíamos	pudemos	pudéramos	pudéssemos	pudermos	
(poderíeis)	(pudestes)	(pudéreis)	(pudésseis)	(puderdes)	(podei)
poderiam	puderam	puderam	pudessem	puderem	

INFINITIVE IMPERSONAL & PERSONAL	GERUND AND PAST PARTICIPLE	PRESENT INDICATIVE	PRESENT SUBJUNCTIVE	IMPERFECT INDICATIVE	FUTURE INDICATIVE
175. pôr *to put, place*					
pôr	pọndo	pọnho	pọnha	pụnha	porẹi
(pọres)		(pões)	(pọnhas)	(pụnhas)	(porás)
pôr		põe	pọnha	pụnha	porá
pọrmos	pôsto, pọsta, pọstos, pọstas	pọmos	ponhạmos	púnhamos	porẹmos
(pọrdes)		(pọndes)	(ponhạis)	(púnheis)	(porẹis)
pọrem		põem and põe	pọnham	pụnham	porãо
176. querẹr *to wish*					
querẹr	querẹndo	quẹro	quẹira	querịa	quererẹi
(querẹres)		(quẹres)	(quẹiras)	(querịas)	(quererás)
querẹr		quẹre, quẹr	quẹira	querịa	quererá
querẹrmos	querịdo	querẹmos	queirạmos	queríamos	quererẹmos
(querẹrdes)		(querẹis)	(queirạis)	(queríeis)	(quererẹis)
querẹrem		quẹrem	quẹiram	querịam	quererãо
177. rịr *to laugh*					
rịr	rịndo	rịo	rịa	rịa	rirẹi
(rịres)		(rịs)	(rịas)	(rịas)	(rirás)
rịr		rị	rịa	rịa	rirá
rịrmos	rịdo	rịmos	riạmos	ríamos	rirẹmos
(rịrdes)		(rịdes)	(riạis)	(ríeis)	(rirẹis)
rịrem		rịem	rịam	rịam	rirãо
178. sabẹr *to know*					
sabẹr	sabẹndo	sẹi	sạiba	sabịa	saberẹi
(sabẹres)		(sạbes)	(sạibas)	(sabịas)	(saberás)
sabẹr		sạbe	sạiba	sabịa	saberá
sabẹrmos	sabịdo	sabẹmos	saibạmos	sabíamos	saberẹmos
(sabẹrdes)		(sabẹis)	(saibạis)	(sabíeis)	(saberẹis)
sabẹrem		sạbem	sạibam	sabịam	saberãо

CONDITIONAL	PRETERIT INDICATIVE	PLUPERFECT INDICATIVE	IMPERFECT SUBJUNCTIVE	FUTURE SUBJUNCTIVE	IMPERATIVE
porįa	pųs	pusęra	pusęsse	pusęr	
(porįas)	(pusęste)	(pusęras)	(pusęsses)	(pusęres)	(pǫe)
porįa	pôs	pusęra	pusęsse	pusęr	
porįamos	pusęmos	puséramos	puséssemos	pusęrmos	
(porįeis)	(pusęstes)	(puséreis)	(pusésseis)	(pusęrdes)	(pǫnde)
porįam	pusęram	pusęram	pusęssem	pusęrem	
quererįa	quįs	quisęra	quisęsse	quisęr	
(quererįas)	(quisęste)	(quisęras)	(quisęsses)	(quisęres)	(quęr) (quęre)
quererįa	quįs	quisęra	quisęsse	quisęr	
quereríamos	quisęmos	quiséramos	quiséssemos	quisęrmos	
(quereríeis)	(quisęstes)	(quiséreis)	(quisésseis)	(quisęrdes)	(queręi)
quererįam	quisęram	quisęram	quisęssem	quisęrem	
ririą	rį	rįra	rįsse	rįr	
(ririas)	(rįste)	(rįras)	(rįsses)	(rįres)	(rį)
ririą	rįu	rįra	rįsse	rįr	
riríamos	rįmos	ríramos	ríssemos	rįrmos	
(riríeis)	(rįstes)	(ríreis)	(rísseis)	(rįrdes)	(rįde)
ririąm	rįram	rįram	rįssem	rįrem	
saberįa	sǫube	soubęra	soubęsse	soubęr	
(saberįas)	(soubęste)	(soubęras)	(soubęsses)	(soubęres)	(sąbe)
saberįa	sǫube	soubęra	soubęsse	soubęr	
saberíamos	soubęmos	soubéramos	soubéssemos	soubęrmos	
(saberíeis)	(soubęstes)	(soubéreis)	(soubésseis)	(soubęrdes)	(sabęi)
saberįam	soubęram	soubęram	soubęssem	soubęrem	

INFINITIVE IMPERSONAL & PERSONAL	GERUND AND PAST PARTICIPLE	PRESENT INDICATIVE	PRESENT SUBJUNCTIVE	IMPERFECT INDICATIVE	FUTURE INDICATIVE
179. saịr *to go out*					
saịr	saịndo	sạio	sạia	saía	saïrẹi
(saíres)		(sạis)	(sạias)	(saías)	(saïrás)
saịr	saído	sại	sạia	saía	saïrá
saírmos		saímos	saiạmos	saíamos	saïrẹmos
(saírdes)		(saís)	(saiạis)	(saíeis)	(saïrẹis)
saírem		sạem	sạiam	saíam	saïrą̃o
180. sẹr *to be*					
sẹr	sẹndo	sọu	sẹja	ẹra	serẹi
(sẹres)		(és)	(sẹjas)	(ẹras)	(serás)
sẹr	sịdo	é	sẹja	ẹra	será
sẹrmos		sọmos	sejạmos	éramos	serẹmos
(sẹrdes)		(sọis)	(sejạis)	(éreis)	(serẹis)
sẹrem		são	sẹjam	ẹram	serą̃o
181. tẹr *to have*					
tẹr	tẹndo	tẹnho	tẹnha	tịnha	terẹi
(tẹres)		(tẹns)	(tẹnhas)	(tịnhas)	(terás)
tẹr	tịdo	tẹm	tẹnha	tịnha	terá
tẹrmos		tẹmos	tenhạmos	tínhamos	terẹmos
(tẹrdes)		(tẹndes)	(tenhạis)	(tínheis)	(terẹis)
tẹrem		tẹem and têm	tẹnham	tịnham	terą̃o
182. trazẹr *to bring*					
trazẹr	trazẹndo	trạgo	trạga	trazịa	trarẹi
(trazẹres)		(trạzes)	(trạgas)	(trazịas)	(trarás)
trazẹr	trazịdo	trạz	trạga	trazịa	trará
trazẹrmos		trazẹmos	tragạmos	trazíamos	trarẹmos
(trazẹrdes)		(trazẹis)	(tragạis)	(trazíeis)	(trarẹis)
trazẹrem		trạzem	trạgam	trazịam	trarą̃o

CONDITIONAL	PRETERIT INDICATIVE	PLUPERFECT INDICATIVE	IMPERFECT SUBJUNCTIVE	FUTURE SUBJUNCTIVE	IMPERATIVE
saïrįa	saí	saíra	saísse	saįr	
(saïrįas)	(saíste)	(saíras)	(saísses)	(saíres)	(saįi)
saïrįa	saíu	saíra	saísse	saįr	
saïríamos	saímos	saíramos	saíssemos	saírmos	
(saïríeis)	(saístes)	(saíreis)	(saísseis)	(saírdes)	(saí)
saïrįam	saíram	saíram	saíssem	saírem	
serįa	fui	fôra	fǫsse	for	
(serįas)	(fǫste)	(fǫras)	(fǫsses)	(fǫres)	(sê)
serįa	fǫi	fôra	fǫsse	for	
seríamos	fǫmos	fôramos	fôssemos	fǫrmos	
(seríeis)	(fǫstes)	(fôreis)	(fôsseis)	(fǫrdes)	(sêde)
serįam	fǫram	fǫram	fǫssem	fǫrem	
terįa	tįve	tivęra	tivęsse	tivęr	
(terįas)	(tivęste)	(tivęras)	(tivęsses)	(tivęres)	(tęm)
terįa	tęve	tivęra	tivęsse	tivęr	
teríamos	tivęmos	tivéramos	tivéssemos	tivęrmos	
(teríeis)	(tivęstes)	(tivéreis)	(tivésseis)	(tivęrdes)	(tęnde)
terįam	tivęram	tivęram	tivęssem	tivęrem	
trarįa	trǫuxe [1]	trouxęra	trouxęsse	trouxęr	
(trarįas)	(trouxęste)	(trouxęras)	(trouxęsses)	(trouxęres)	(trąz) (trąze)
trarįa	trǫuxe	trouxęra	trouxęsse	trouxęr	
traríamos	trouxęmos	trouxéramos	trouxéssemos	trouxęrmos	
(traríeis)	(trouxęstes)	(trouxéreis)	(trouxésseis)	(trouxęrdes)	(trazęi)
trarįam	trouxęram	trouxęram	trouxęssem	trouxęrem	

[1] The *x* of this tense and the derived tenses is pronounced like *ss* (section 45 b).

INFINITIVE IMPERSONAL & PERSONAL	GERUND AND PAST PARTICIPLE	PRESENT INDICATIVE	PRESENT SUBJUNCTIVE	IMPERFECT INDICATIVE	FUTURE INDICATIVE
183. valẹr *to be worth*					
valẹr	valẹndo	vạlho	vạlha	valịa	valerẹi
(valẹres)		(vạles)	(vạlhas)	(valịas)	(valerás)
valẹr		vạle	vạlha	valịa	valerá
valẹrmos	valịdo	valẹmos	valhạmos	valíamos	valerẹmos
(valẹrdes)		(valẹis)	(valhạis)	(valíeis)	(valerẹis)
valẹrem		vạlem	vạlham	valịam	valerãọ
184. vẹr *to see*					
vẹr	vẹndo	vẹjo	vẹja	vịa	verẹi
(vẹres)		(vês)	(vẹjas)	(vịas)	(verás)
vẹr		vê	vẹja	vịa	verá
vẹrmos	vịsto	vẹmos	vejạmos	víamos	verẹmos
(vẹrdes)		(vêdes)	(vejạis)	(víeis)	(verẹis)
vẹrem		vêem	vẹjam	vịam	verãọ
185. vịr *to come*					
vịr	vịndo	vẹnho	vẹnha	vịnha	virẹi
(vịres)		(vẹns)	(vẹnhas)	(vịnhas)	(virás)
vịr		vẹm	vẹnha	vịnha	virá
vịrmos	vịndo	vịmos	venhạmos	vínhamos	virẹmos
(vịrdes)		(vịndes)	(venhạis)	(vínheis)	(virẹis)
vịrem		vẹem and vêm	vẹnham	vịnham	virãọ

CONDITIONAL	PRETERIT INDICATIVE	PLUPERFECT INDICATIVE	IMPERFECT SUBJUNCTIVE	FUTURE SUBJUNCTIVE	IMPERATIVE
valeria	valí	valęra	valęsse	valęr	
(valerias)	(valęste)	(valęras)	(valęsses)	(valęres)	(vąle)
valeria	valęu	valęra	valęsse	valęr	
valeríamos	valęmos	valêramos	valêssemos	valęrmos	
(valeríeis)	(valęstes)	(valêreis)	(valêsseis)	(valęrdes)	(valęi)
valeriam	valęram	valęram	valęssem	valęrem	
veria	ví	vira	visse	vir	
(verias)	(viste)	(viras)	(visses)	(vires)	(vê)
veria	viu	vira	visse	vir	
veríamos	vimos	víramos	víssemos	virmos	
(veríeis)	(vistes)	(víreis)	(vísseis)	(virdes)	(vêde)
veriam	viram	viram	vissem	virem	
viria	vim	vięra	vięsse	vięr	
(virias)	(vięste)	(vięras)	(vięsses)	(vięres)	(vęm)
viria	vęio	vięra	vięsse	vięr	
viríamos	vięmos	viéramos	viéssemos	vięrmos	
(viríeis)	(vięstes)	(viéreis)	(viésseis)	(vięrdes)	(vinde)
viriam	vięram	vięram	vięssem	vięrem	

Portuguese-English Vocabulary

The numbers refer to sections.

a to, for, into, at
a *f. art.* the; *pron.* her, it
à = **a** + **a** to the
abẹrto -a open
abril *m.* April
abrir to open
acabạr to end, terminate, finish; — **por** to finish by; — **de** to have just; **acabava de** had just
aceitạr to accept
acẹito *p.p. of* **aceitar**
acendẹr to light
acentuạr (158, 3) to accent
acidẹnte *m.* accident
achạr to find
aconselhạr (a que) (155, 5) to advise; — **a** to advise to
acordạr to get awake
Açôres *m. pl.* Azores
acostumạr-se a to accustom oneself to
acreditạr to believe
actọr *m.* (**c** *silent*) actor
acusạr de to charge with
adormecẹr (154; 155, 2) to go to sleep
advogạdo *m.* lawyer
afastạr-se to move away, go away
a-fim que so that, in order that
agọra now; — **que** now that
agôsto *m.* August
água *f.* water
aí there (*near the person spoken to*); — **por** about
ainda still, yet; — **que** although
ajudạr (a) to help (to)
alẹgre gay, merry
além de besides
alemão -ã -ães German
alfaiatarịa *f.* tailor shop
alfaiạte *m.* tailor
algibẹira *f.* pocket
algụm, algụma some; *see* **coisa** *and* **vez**

alị there (*near the person or thing spoken of*); **por** — that way
almôço, almọços *m.* (135) lunch; **pequẹno** — breakfast
ạlto -a tall, high
alugạr (150) to rent
alumiạr (158, 2) to illuminate, light up
aluno *m.* pupil, student
àmanhã tomorrow; — **de manhã** tomorrow morning; — **de tạrde** tomorrow afternoon
ạmbos -as both
América *f.* America
americạno -a American
amigo *m.* friend
amọstra *f.* sample
andạr *m.* floor; **primẹiro** — second floor
animạl *m.* animal
ạno *m.* year; *see* **dia** *and* **ter**
ạntes *adv.* before; — **de** before *prep.*; — **que** before *conj.*; **quanto** — as soon as possible
ao = **a** + **o** to the
aos = **a** + **os** to the
apagạr (150) to put out, extinguish
apanhạr to pick up
apẹnas only
a-pesạr-de in spite of
aplicạdo -a studious
aprendẹr (a) to learn (to)
apresentạr to introduce
apressạr-se (a) (155, 1) to hurry (to)
aquêle, aquẹla (66) that, that one (yonder), those
aquí here; **por** — this way
aquịlo (67) that
ạr *m.* air
artịsta *m. & f.* artist
artigo *m.* article
árvore *f.* tree
as *f. pl. art.* the; *pron.* them

149

às = a + as to the
assegurar to assure
assim so, thus; — que as soon as; não
  é — ? is it not so?
assunto m. subject, affair
até prep. until; — que conj. until
atento -a attentive
atrás de behind
aula f. classroom
ausente absent
automóvel m. automobile
ave f. bird
avenida f. avenue
avião, aviões m. airplane
azul, azuis blue

banho m. bath, bathing; see fato and
  tomar
barato -a cheap; barato adv. cheap,
  cheaply
barbear (158, 1) to shave
bastante enough
beber (155, 2) to drink
beira-mar f. seashore
belo -a beautiful
bem well
biblioteca f. library
bilhete m. ticket
boa f. of bom
bocadinho m. little bit; little while
bôlsa f. pocketbook
bom, boa good, kind
bondade f. kindness
bonde m. (Brazilian) trolley car, streetcar; see linhas
branco -a white
Brasil m. Brazil
brasileiro -a Brazilian
breve brief; adv. shortly, presently;
  em — soon

cá here
caber (159) to fit; to be contained
cachimbo m. pipe
cada each, every
cadeira f. chair
café m. coffee; — da manhã m. (Brazilian) breakfast

cair (160) to fall
calar-se to be silent, keep quiet
calçada f. (Brazilian) sidewalk
calor m. heat; see fazer and ter
cama f. bed; see ir
caminhar to walk
camisa f. shirt
campo m. country
cansado -a tired
cansar-se de to get tired of
cantar to sing
cão, cães m. dog
capital f. capital (city)
carne f. meat
caro -a dear; caro adv. dear
carril m. track; carris de ferro trolley
  lines
carro eléctrico m. (c of ct silent) trolley
  car, streetcar
carta f. letter
casa f. house; — de campo country
  house; — de hóspedes boardinghouse; — vizinha house next door;
  em — at home, home; em — de at
  the house of; a —, para — home; a —
  de to the house of, to the home of; see
  chegar, ir, sair, and voltar
casar(-se) to get married
caso m. case; (no) — (que) in case
  (that)
catorze fourteen
cavalo m. horse
cedinho pretty early
cedo early
cego -a blind
célebre famous
cem a hundred
cento hundred, a hundred
centro m. center
certo -a sure
cessar de to stop
céu m. sky, heaven
chá m. tea
chamada f. call; fazer a — to call the
  roll
chamar to call; mandar — to send for;
  —-se to be called; chamo-me my
  name is

chão *m.* floor, ground
chapéu *m.* hat
charuto *m.* cigar
chave *f.* key
chegada *f.* arrival
chegar (150) to arrive; — a casa to arrive home; — a to amount to; — para to be enough to *or* for
cheio -a full
cheiro *m.* odor
chover (156, 2) to rain
cidade *f.* city
cigarro *m.* cigarette
cinco five
cinema *m.* movie, motion pictures
civil, civis civil
classe *f.* class
clima *m.* climate
coberto -a covered
coisa *f.* thing; alguma — something
Colombo *m.* Columbus
com with
combóio *m.* train
começar (153; 155, 1) to begin; — por to begin by
comer (156, 2) to eat
comércio *m.* business, commerce
comigo with me
como how; as; tão . . . — as . . . as
cômo *1st sg. pres. ind. of* comer
companhia *f.* company
compor (175) to compose
comum, comuns common
compra *f.* purchase; *see* fazer and ir
comprar to buy
concêrto, concertos *m.* concert
confiança *f.* confidence, trust
conhecer (154; 155, 2) to know
connosco with us
conseguir (152; 155, 3) to get, obtain
consertar (155, 1) to mend, repair
consigo with himself, with herself, with itself, with yourself, with themselves, with yourselves, with you
conta *f.* bill
contanto que provided (that)
contar to count; to tell; to intend; to expect

contente content, satisfied; — em *or* de glad to; ficar — to be glad
contigo with thee
continuar (158, 3) to continue
conveniente convenient
conversa *f.* conversation
conversar (155, 1) to converse
convidar a *or* para to invite to
convite *m.* invitation
convosco with you
copiar (158, 2) to copy
copo *m.* glass, tumbler
côr *f.* color
correctamente (c *of* ct *silent*) correctly
correio *m.* mail; *see* sêlo
corrigir (151) to correct
cortês polite
crer (161) to believe, think; — que sim to think so; — que não to think not
criada *f.* maid
criado *m.* servant, waiter
cujo -a whose, of whom, of which
culpadinho somewhat to blame
custar to cost

da = de + a from the
dançar to dance
daquela = de + aquela of that
daquêle = de + aquêle of that
daquilo = de + aquilo of that
dar (162) to give; to strike; — com to encounter, run into; — para to overlook; to face; — um passeio to take a walk
das = de + as of the
de of, from, by, with
decidir to decide (to); — -se a to decide to
décimo -a tenth
de-fronte across the street
deitar-se to lie down, go to bed
deixar to let, allow to; — de to stop, cease
dela = de + ela of her, of it
dêle = de + êle of him, of it
delicioso, deliciosa (136) delightful
demais too, too much; os — the rest, the others

demasiado too, too much
demora f. delay
depois adv. afterwards; — de prep. after; — que conj. after
de-pressa fast
descanso m. rest
descer to go down; — de to get off or out of (a vehicle)
descoberta f. discovery
descoberto -a p.p. of descobrir
descobridor m. discoverer
descobrir (156, 3) to discover
desejar (155, 5) to wish, desire
despir-se (155, 3) to undress
dessa = de + essa of that
dêsse = de + êsse of that
desta = de + esta of this
dêste = de + êste of this
de-vagar slow, slowly
de-vagarinho slow and easy
dever (155, 2) to owe; to have to, be bound to, must
dez ten
dezanove nineteen
dezasseis sixteen
dezassete seventeen
dezembro m. december
dezenove (Brazilian) nineteen
dezesseis (Brazilian) sixteen
dezessete (Brazilian) seventeen
dezóito eighteen
dia m. day; — de anos birthday; oito —s a week; quinze —s two weeks; —s úteis workdays
diante de in front of
diferente different
difícil, difíceis difficult, hard
dinheiro m. money
direito -a right; direito adv. straight
disso = de + isso of that
disto = de + isto of this
divertir-se (155, 3) to enjoy oneself
dizer (163) to say, tell; querer — to mean; ouvir — que to hear that
do = de + o of the
doce sweet, gentle
doente sick, ill

dois, duas two
domingo m. Sunday
donde from where
dormir (156, 3) to sleep; quarto de —. bedroom
dos = de + os of the
doze twelve
duas f. of dois two
dum = de + um of a
duma = de + uma of a
dúvida f. doubt; sem — doubtless
duvidar to doubt
duzentos -as two hundred

e and
ela she, her, it
êle he, him, it
eléctrico -a (c of ct silent) electric; see carro
elementar elementary
em in, into, on, at
embora although; see ir
empregado m. clerk, salesman
emprestar to lend
encarregar to load, entrust; — -se de to take charge of
encetar (155, 1) to begin, establish
endereço m. address
enquanto (que) while
ensejo m. opportunity
ensinar (a) to teach (to)
então then
entrar em to enter, go or come into
entre between, among
entregar (155, 1) to deliver
entregue p.p. of entregar
enviar (158, 2) to send
escada f. stairs
escola f. school
escrever (155, 2) to write
escrito -a written
escritor m. writer
escutar to listen to
Espanha f. Spain
espanhol, espanhola, espanhóis Spanish
espécie f. kind
espelho m. mirror

●sperar (155, 1) to hope (to); to wait, wait for, await
esquecer(-se de) (p. 93, note 3; 154) to forget (to)
esquerdo -a left
esquina f. corner
êsse, essa (66) that, that one (*near you*), those
esta f. *of* êste
estação, estações f. station; season; — balnear bathing resort; — final terminus
Estados Unidos m. pl. United States
estante f. bookcase
estar (164) to be; — com fome to be hungry; — com sêde to be thirsty; — de volta to be back; — com vontade de to have a mind to, wish to
êste, esta (66) this, this one, these
estrada f. road
estreito -a narrow
estudar to study
eu I
Europa f. Europe
examinar to examine
Excelência f. Excellency; Vossa — Your Excellency, you
excelente excellent
excursão, excursões f. trip
exemplo m. example
exercício m. exercise
êxito m. success

fácil, fáceis easy
falar to speak
faltar a to be absent from
famoso, famosa (136) famous
farmácia f. drugstore
fato m. suit (of clothes); — de banho bathing suit
favor m. favor; faz — de please
fazenda f. cloth
fazer (165) to do; to make; que tempo faz? how is the weather?; faz bom tempo it (the weather) is fine; faz mau tempo it (the weather) is bad; faz calor it is hot *or* warm; faz frio it is cold; faz vento it is windy; — a

chamada to call the roll; — uma pregunta to ask a question; ir — compras (*Brazilian*) to go shopping; faz favor de please
febre f. fever
fechar (155, 5) to close
feliz happy
férias grandes f. pl. summer holiday, summer vacation
ferro m. iron
fevereiro m. February
ficar (149) to stay, remain; to be; — contente to be glad
Filadélfia f. Philadelphia
filha f. daughter
filho m. son
flor f. flower
fogo, fogos m. (135) fire
folgar de (156, 5) to be glad to
fome f. hunger; *see* estar *and* ter
fora outside
formoso, formosa (136) beautiful
francês -a French
frase f. sentence
freguês m. customer
fresco -a fresh; de fresco freshly
frio -a cold; *see* fazer *and* ter
fumar to smoke

ganhar (note 1, p. 118) to earn
ganho p.p. *of* ganhar
garçon m. (*Brazilian*) waiter
gastar to spend
gasto p.p. *of* gastar
gaveta f. drawer
gêlo m. ice
gente f. people; tôda a — everybody
geralmente generally
glorioso, gloriosa (136) glorious
gostar de (156, 1) to like (to)
gozar to enjoy
grande large, big, great
grandes férias f. pl. (*Brazilian*) summer holiday, summer vacation
gravata f. necktie
grupo m. group
guarda-chuva m. umbrella

há there is, there are; ago
haver (166) to have
hesitar em to hesitate to
história *f.* history
hoje today
homem *m.* man
hora *f.* hour; time, o'clock
hóspede *m.* guest; *see* **casa**
hotel, hotéis *m.* hotel

igreja *f.* church
igual, iguais a like, similar to
ilha *f.* island
imediatamente at once, immediately, right away
imperador *m.* emperor
importante important
importar (156, 1) to be important to
inglês, inglêsa, inglêses, inglêsas English
interessante interesting
interessar to interest
inverno *m.* winter
ir (167) to go; — **para casa** to go home; — **para a cama** to go to bed; — **às compras** to go shopping; — **-se (embora)** to go away; — **a pé** to walk; — **ter com** to go to, go to see; to apply to; — **fazer compras** (*Brazilian*) to go shopping; **vamos** + *infinitive* let us . . .
irmã *f.* sister
irmão, irmãos *m.* brother
isso (67) that
isto (67) this; **por** — therefore

já already, now, at once; — **não** no longer
janeiro *m.* January
janela *f.* window
jantar *m.* dinner; **sala de** — dining room
jardim *m.* garden
jazer (168) to lie
João *m.* John
jornal *m.* newspaper
José *m.* Joseph
jovem, jovens young
julho *m.* July

junho *m.* June
juntos -as together

-la her, it
lã *f.* wool
lado *m.* side; **de . . . —** on . . . side
lâmpada *f.* lamp, light
lápis *m.* pencil
lembrar-se de to remember (to)
lente *m.* professor
ler (169) to read
levantar-se to rise, get up
levar (155, 1) to take (away); to wear; to take (*of time*)
lhe to him, to her, to it
lhes to them
lha = **lhe** + **a** it to him, it to her, it to them, it to you
lho = **lhe** + **o** it to him, it to her, it to them, it to you
lição, lições *f.* lesson
liçãozinha *f.* little bit of a lesson
licença *f.* permission; **com** — I beg your pardon
lindo -a pretty
língua *f.* language
linhas de bonde *f. pl.* (*Brazilian*) trolley lines
Lisboa *f.* Lisbon
livraria *f.* bookstore
livro *m.* book
-lo him, it
logo right away; — **que** as soon as
loja *f.* store
longe (de) far (from)
-los them
lugar *m.* place
Luiz Louis
luva *f.* glove
luz *f.* light

ma = **me** + **a** it to me
má *f. of* **mau**
mãe *f.* mother
magoado -a sore
maio *m.* May
maior larger, greater; *see* **parte**

mais more, most; **não** . . . — no . . . longer

mal badly, poorly; ill

mandar to order; to have, cause to; — **chamar** to send for

manhã *f.* morning

mão, mãos *f.* hand

mar *m.* sea

março *m.* March

mas but

más *f. pl. of* mau

materno -a maternal, mother

mau, má bad, unkind; naughty; poor

me me, to me

medicina *f.* medicine

médico *m.* physician, doctor

medir (170) to measure

mêdo *m.* fear; **ter — de** to be afraid of *or* to

meia half past

meia-noite *f.* midnight, twelve o'clock

meio-dia *m.* noon, twelve o'clock

melhor better, best

mendigo *m.* beggar

menor smaller, smallest

menos less, least, fewer, fewest; **a —** **que** unless

mentira *f.* lie

mês, meses *m.* month

mesa *f.* table

mesmo -a same

meter-se a to begin to

meu minha my, mine

mil thousand, a thousand

milhão, milhões *m.* million

mim me

minha *f. of* meu

minuto *m.* minute

mo = me + o it to me

moça *f.* (*Brazilian*) girl

mocidade *f.* youth

modo *m.* way, manner, mood; **de — que** so that

morar (156, 1) to live, dwell

morrer (156, 2) to die; **— de** to die of; to languish with

morto, morta (136) *p.p. of* morrer

mostrar (156, 1) to show

mover (156, 2) to move

mudar-se to move

muitíssimo very much

muito -a much, many; **muito** *adv.* very, much, hard, a great deal; **— . . .** **para** too . . . to; **muitas vezes** often

mundo *m.* world; **todo o —** (*Brazilian*) everybody

música *f.* music

na = em + a in the

-na her, it

nada nothing; **não** . . . — nothing, not anything

nadar to swim

não no, not; **— . . . nada** nothing, not anything; **também —** not either, neither; **— . . . mais** no longer, not any longer; **— . . . senão** only, nothing but; **já —** no longer; **a — ser** **que** unless; *see* crer

naquela = em + aquela in that

naquêle = em + aquêle in that

nas = em + as in the

nascimento *m.* birth

nela = em + ela in it, in her

nêle = em + êle in it, in him

nem . . . **nem** neither . . . nor

nenhum, nenhuma no, not any

nessa = em + essa in that

nêsse = em + êsse in that

nesta = em + esta in this

nêste = em + êste in this

ninguém no one, nobody

nisso = em + isso in that

nisto = em + isto in this

no = em + o in the

-no him, it

noite *f.* night, evening; **esta —** this evening, tonight; *see* ontem

no-la = nos + a it to us

no-lo = nos + o it to us

nome *m.* name

nono -a ninth

nos = em + os in the

nos us, to us

nós us

nosso -a our, ours

notícia *f.* news; *see* **ter**
Nova York New York
nove nine
novecentos -as nine hundred
novembro *m.* November
noventa ninety
novo, nova (136) new, recent, young
num = em + um in a
numa = em + uma in a
número *m.* number
nunca never

o *m. art.* the; *pron.* him, it; **o que** (**a que, os que, as que**) he who (she who, the one who, those who, the ones who, he whom, the one which, the one that); **o que** *neut.* what, that which; **o de** (**a de, os de, as de**) that of (those of)
obra *f.* work
obrigado -a thanks, thank you; **muito — ** many thanks
obrigar a to oblige to
oitavo -a eighth
oitenta eighty
Oceano Atlântico *m.* Atlantic Ocean
oito eight; **— dias** a week
oitocentos -as eight hundred
ôlho, olhos *m.* (135) eye
onde where; **para —** where, whither; **por —** which way
ontem yesterday; **— à noite** last evening, last night; **— à tarde** yesterday afternoon
onze eleven
ou or
outono *m.* autumn, fall
outro -a other, another; **um ao —** each other
outubro *m.* October
ouvir (171) to hear; **— dizer que** to hear that
ôvo, ovos *m.* (135) egg

pacote *m.* package
pàdeiro *m.* baker
pagar (150) to pay
pago *p.p. of* **pagar**
pai *m.* father

país *m.* country
palavra *f.* word
pão, pães *m.* bread, loaf of bread
papel, papéis *m.* paper, document
para for, to, towards; **— que** so that, in order that
paragem *f.* stop; **— central** terminus
parar de to stop
parecer (154; 155, 2) to seem (to), look; to suit; **— -se com** to resemble
parque *m.* park
parte *f.* part; **a maior —** the majority, the most
partir to leave, go away
passado -a last
passar to spend; **— sem** to do without
passeio *m.* walk; sidewalk; *see* **dar**
passo: ao — que while, whereas
pé *m.* foot; *see* **ir**
pedir (172) to ask for, request; **— para** to ask to
pedra *f.* stone
pela = por + a by the
pelo = por + o by the
pena *f.* pen; trouble, pain; **é — (que)** it is a pity (that); **ter — ** to be sorry; **valer a —** to be worth while
pensão, pensões *f.* (*Brazilian*) boardinghouse
pensar to intend to; to think; **— em** to think of
pequeno -a small, little
perceber (155, 2) to understand
perder (173) to lose; to miss
perguntar *Brazilian and colloquial for* **preguntar**
permitir to permit (to)
pertencer to belong
perto (de) near
pesar (155, 1) to weigh
pessoa *f.* person
pintar to paint
pianista *m. & f.* pianist
piano *m.* piano
pior worse, worst
pires *m.* saucer
pobre poor
poder (174) to be able (to), **can**

pois well
por by, for, after, because of; **aí —** about
pôr (175) to put, place; to put on; **— -se a** to begin to
porque because
porquê why
porta f. door
pôrto, portos m. (135) harbor, port
Pôrto: o Pôrto Oporto; **vinho do Pôrto** Port wine
Portugal m. Portugal
português, portuguesa Portuguese; **o português** the Portuguese
possível possible
pôsto, posta p.p. of **pôr**; **pôsto que** although
pouco -a little; **poucos -as** few; **pouco** adv. little; **um —** a little
poupar to save
povo, povos m. (135) people
praça f. public square
praia f. beach
prato m. plate
prazer m. pleasure
precisar de to need; **to need to**
preciso -a necessary
prédio m. building, property
preferir (155, 3) to prefer (to)
pergunta f. question; see **fazer**
perguntar to ask; **— por** to ask for
prelo m. printing press; **no —** in press
preparar to prepare; **— -se a** or **para** to prepare to, get ready to
presenciar (158, 1) to witness, be present at
presente present
pressa f. hurry, haste, speed; see **ter**
primavera f. spring
primeiro -a first
procurar to look for, seek; to try to
professor m. professor
proïbir to prohibit, forbid (to)
prometer (155, 2) to promise (to)
pronto -a ready
pronúncia f. pronunciation
pronunciar (158, 2) to pronounce
prova f. proof

provável probable
próximo -a (x = ss) next
publicação f. publication

quadrado -a square
qual, quais what, which; **o qual** who, whom
quando when
quanto all that, everything that; **— antes** as soon as possible; **— tempo** how long
quantos -as all those who; how many
quarenta forty
quarta f. Wednesday
quarta-feira f. Wednesday
quarto m. room; quarter (of an hour); **— de dormir** bedroom; **quarto -a** fourth
quatro four
quatrocentos -as four hundred
que what; who, whom; that; **o — what**, that which; he who, the one who
quem who, whom; **de —** whose
quente hot
querer (176) to wish (to), want (to), will; **— dizer** to mean
quilo m. kilogram
quinhentos -as five hundred
quinta f. Thursday
quinta-feira f. Thursday
quinto -a fifth
quinze fifteen; **— dias** two weeks

rapariga f. girl
rapaz m. boy
ràpidamente quickly, rapidly
razão f. reason; see **ter**
recear (158, 1) to fear (to)
recreio m. recreation, change
redondo -a round
refeição, refeicões f. meal
rei m. king
relógio m. clock
repetir (155, 3) to repeat
rés-do-chão m. ground floor
resolver-se a to decide to
responder to answer
rico -a rich

Rio (de Janeiro) *m.* Rio de Janeiro
rir (177) to laugh; — de to laugh at
romper to break; to tear
roupa de banho *f.* (*Brazilian*) bathing
    suit
rua *f.* street

sã *f. of* são
sábado *m.* Saturday
saber (178) to know; to learn, find out
    about; to know how to, be able to
sair (179) to go out, come out, appear;
    — de casa to go out of the house,
    leave the house
sala *f.* room; — de jantar dining room
são, sã healthy
sapato *m.* shoe
saudades *f. pl.* longing; *see* ter
se if; himself, herself, itself, yourself,
    themselves, yourselves
sêde *f.* thirst; *see* estar *and* ter
séde *f.* seat
segrêdo, segredos *m.* secret
seguinte following
seguir (152; 155, 3) to follow
segunda *f.* Monday
segunda-feira *f.* Monday
segundo -a second
seis six
seiscentos -as six hundred
sêlo do correio *m.* postage stamp
sem without; — que *conj.* without; *see*
    passar
semana *f.* week
sempre always; — que provided (that)
senão: não . . . — only, nothing but
senhor *m.* gentleman; sir; you
senhora *f.* lady; Mrs.; young lady, miss
    (*in Portugal*); you
senhorita *f.* (*Brazilian*) young lady,
    miss; you
sentado -a seated
sentar-se to sit down, seat oneself
sentir (155, 4) to be sorry; to smell
ser (180) to be; a não — que unless
servir (155, 3) to serve
sessenta sixty
sete seven

setecentos -as seven hundred
setembro *m.* September
setenta seventy
sétimo -a seventh
seu, sua his, her, hers, your, yours,
    their, theirs
sexta *f.* Friday
sexta-feira *f.* Friday
sexto -a sixth
si himself, herself, itself, yourself, them-
    selves, yourselves; you; if (*Brazilian*)
sim yes; *see* crer
simples simple
só only, alone, single
sôbre on, about
soldado *m.* (*close* o) soldier
solteiro -a (*close* o) single, unmarried
som *m.* sound
sòmente only
sono *m.* sleep; *see* ter
sòzinho -a all alone
sua *f. of* seu
subir (157, 1) to go up, come up; —
    para to get on *or* into (*a vehicle*)
surpreender (*first* e = *y*) to surprise

ta = te + a it to thee
tabacaria *f.* cigar store
talvez perhaps
também also, too; — não not either,
    neither
tanto -a so much, so many; tanto *adv.*
    so much; tantas vezes so often
tão so; — . . . como as . . . as
tardar a to be long in
tarde *f.* afternoon, evening; *adv.* late;
    see àmanhã *and* ontem
te thee, to thee
teatro *m.* theater
telha *f.* tile
telhado *m.* roof
temer (155, 2) to fear (to), be afraid (to)
tempo *m.* time; weather; é — (de) it is
    time (to); muito — a long time;
    quanto — how long; *see* fazer *and* ter
tencionar to intend to
ter to have, possess; quantos anos tem
    . . . ? how old is . . . ?; — . . .

anos to be . . . years old; — calor to be warm, be hot; — fome to be hungry; — frio to be cold; — mêdo de to be afraid to; — notícias de to hear from; — pena to be sorry; — pressa (de) to be in a hurry (to); — razão to be right; — saudades de to long for, be homesick for, miss; — sêde to be thirsty; — sono to be sleepy; — tempo para to have the time to; — vontade de to have a notion to, wish to, be anxious to; — que + *infinitive* to have to; — + *noun* + para to have . . . to; ir — com to go to, go to see, apply to; vir — com to come to, come to see, apply to

terça *f.* Tuesday

terça-feira *f.* Tuesday

terceiro -a third

terminar to end

terno *m.* (*Brazilian*) suit (of clothes)

teu, tua thy, thine

ti thee

tio *m.* uncle

tirar to take off; to take away, remove; to pull

to = te + o it to thee

todo, tôda all, whole, every; todos everybody; tôda a gente everybody; todo o mundo (*Brazilian*) everybody

tomar (156, 1) to get; to take; — um banho de mar to go bathing in the ocean

tornar (156, 1) to return; to become; — a to . . . again

tôrre *f.* tower

tossir (156, 3) to cough

trabalhar to work

trabalho *m.* work

travessia *f.* crossing

trazer (182) to bring

trem *m.* (*Brazilian*) train

três three

treze thirteen

trezentos -as three hundred

trinta thirty

tu thou

tudo everything, all

tua *f. of* teu

ùltimamente lately, recently

último -a last

um, uma a, an; one; um ao outro each other

unir to unite

universidade *f.* university

útil, úteis useful; *see* dia

vago -a unoccupied, not taken

valer to be worth; — a pena to be worth while

vamos + *infinitive* let us . . .

vários -as several

vélho -a old; o vélho the old man

vender to sell

vento *m.* wind; *see* fazer

ver (184) to see

verão, verões *m.* summer

verdade *f.* truth; é — it is true

verde green

vestir (155, 3 and 5) to put on; — -se to dress (oneself)

vez *f.* time; em — de instead of; algumas vezes sometimes; muitas vezes often; tantas vezes so often

viagem *f.* trip, voyage

viajar to travel

vinho *m.* wine; — do Pôrto Port wine

vinte twenty

violino *m.* violin

vir (185) to come; — a to come to, happen to; — ter com to come to, come to see, apply to

visitar to visit; to look at

vizinho -a neighboring, next door

você (*open* o) you

vo-la = vos + a it to you

vo-lo = vos + o it to you

volta *f.* return; estar de — to be back

voltar (156, 5) to return; — para casa to return home; — a to . . . again

vontade *f.* will, wish; *see* estar *and* ter

vos you, to you

vós you

vosso -a your, yours; *see* Excelência

voz *f.* voice

English-Portuguese Vocabulary

able: to be — poder
absent ausente
address enderêço m.
advise aconselhar (a que)
afraid: to be — (to) temer, ter mêdo
(de)
after prep. depois de; conj. depois que
afternoon tarde f.
again novamente; to . . . — tornar a,
voltar a
ago há
air ar m.
all todo, tôda
allow deixar, permitir
also também
although ainda que
always sempre
American americano -a, norte-americano -a
and e
another outro -a
any algum, alguma; not . . . — não
. . . nenhum
anything alguma coisa; not . . . —
não . . . nada
arrive chegar; to — home chegar a casa
as como; — . . . — tão . . . como
ask (inquire) preguntar; (request) pedir;
to — for preguntar por; pedir; to —
to pedir para or que; to — a question fazer uma pregunta
at em; (in expressions of time) a
automobile automóvel m.
autumn outono m.
avenue avenida f.
awake acordar; to get — acordar
away: to go — ir-se (embora)

back: to be — estar de volta
bad mau, má; see weather
badly mal
baker pàdeiro m.

bathing suit fato de banho m.; roupa
de banho f. (Brazilian)
be ser, estar; it is . . . o'clock são;
(of weather) it is faz; there is, there
are há; see back, cold, glad, hot,
hungry, sleepy, sorry, thirsty, worth,
and year
beautiful formoso -a
because porque
bed cama f.; to go to — deitar-se, ir
para a cama
bedroom quarto de dormir m.
before prep. antes de
begin começar
behind atrás de
believe crer, acreditar
best melhor
better melhor
bill conta f.
birth nascimento m.
bit: a little — um bocadinho
blue azul
book livro m.
bookcase estante f.
bookstore livraria f.
boy rapaz m.
Brazil o Brasil
bread pão m.
breakfast pequeno almôço m.; café da
manhã m. (Brazilian)
bring trazer
brother irmão m.
building prédio m., edifício m.
but mas
buy comprar

call chamar; to — the roll fazer a
chamada
can poder
case caso m.; in — (no) caso (que)
chair cadeira f.
church igreja f.

160

city cidade *f.*
class classe *f.*
clock relógio *m.*; *see* **o'clock**
cold frio; **to be — ter** frio
come vir; **to — down** descer; **to — into** entrar em; **to — up** subir
confidence confiança *f.*
continue continuar
copy copiar
correct corrigir
correctly correctamente
cough tossir
could *pret. and imperf. ind. of* poder
country campo *m.*
customer freguês *m.*

day dia *m.*
deal: a great — muito, muitíssimo
December dezembro *m.*
did you not? não é assim?
difficult difícil
do fazer; **to — without** passar sem
doctor médico *m.*
dog cão *m.*
door porta *f.*; **next —** vizinho -a
doubt duvidar
drawer gaveta *f.*
dress (oneself) vestir-se
drink beber

each cada; **— other** um ao outro, uns aos outros; nos, se
early cedo; **— enough** bastante cedo; **pretty —** cedinho
easy fácil
eat comer
egg ôvo *m.*
eight oito
either: not — também não
eleven onze
emperor imperador *m.*
English inglês, inglêsa
enjoy: to — oneself divertir-se
enough bastante; **early —** bastante cedo
enter entrar em
evening tarde *f.*
every todo, tôda; cada

everybody tôda a gente, todos; todo o mundo (*Brazilian*)
example exemplo *m.*
excellent excelente
exercise exercício *m.*
expect contar, esperar
eye ôlho *m.*

face dar para
fall cair
far (from) longe (de)
fast de-pressa, ràpidamente
father pai *m.*
February fevereiro *m.*
few poucos -as; **fewer** menos
find achar, encontrar; **to — out about** saber
fine bom, boa; *see* **weather**
finish acabar, terminar
five cinco; **— hundred** quinhentos -as
floor andar *m.*
flower flor *f.*
follow seguir
for para
forget esquecer, esquecer-se de
four quatro
French francês, francesa
full cheio -a
Friday sexta *f.*, sexta-feira *f.*
friend amigo *m.*
from de; **— where** donde
front: in — of diante de

garden jardim *m.*
generally geralmente
gentleman senhor *m.*
German alemão, alemã
get tomar; conseguir; **to — awake** acordar; **to — married** casar(-se); **to — off** descer; **to — out of** descer de; **to — ready to** preparar-se a *or* para; **to — tired of** cansar-se de; **to — up** levantar-se
girl rapariga *f.*; moça (*Brazilian*)
give dar
glad: to be — ficar contente
glass copo *m.*
glove luva *f.*

go ir; **to — away** ir-se (embora); **to — to
bed** deitar-se, ir para a cama; **to —
shopping** ir às compras; **to — to sleep**
adormecer; **to — to see** ir ter com;
to — up subir
good bom, boa
great grande; **a — deal** muito, muitíssimo
ground chão *m.*
guest hóspede *m.*

half meio -a; **— past** . . . e meia
happy feliz
harbor pôrto *m.*
hard difícil; *adv.* muito; **harder** mais
hat chapéu *m.*
have ter; (*cause*) mandar; **to — to ter
que; to — + *noun* + to ter . . .
para; to — (the) time to** ter tempo
para; **to — a notion to** ter vontade de,
estar com vontade de; **to — just**
acabar de; **had just** acabava de
he êle
healthy são, sã
hear ouvir; **to — that** ouvir dizer que
help ajudar; **to — to** ajudar a
her *personal pron.* a; ela; **to — lhe, a
ela; *possessive pron. and adj.* seu, sua,
o . . . dela
here aqui, cá; **— is** aqui tem
herself se
hesitate (to) hesitar (em)
him o; êle; **to — lhe; it to — lho, lha;
with — consigo, com êle
himself se
his seu, sua, o . . . dêle
home (*with verbs of motion*) para casa,
a casa; **home** *or* **at home** em casa;
to arrive home chegar a casa
homesick: to be — for ter saudades de
hope esperar
hot quente; **to be — ter** calor
hotel hotel *m.*
house casa *f.*; **the — next door** a casa
vizinha
how como; **— many** quantos -as; **— is
the weather?** que tempo faz?; **— old
is . . . ?** quantos anos tem?; **to

**know — saber
hundred cem; **five — quinhentos
**hungry: to be — ter fome, estar com
fome
hurry apressar-se

I eu
if se; si (*Brazilian*)
important importante
in em; **— a num, numa; — the no, na,
nos, nas, (*after a superlative*) do, da,
dos, das
instead of em vez de
intend contar, pensar, tencionar
it o, a; -lo, -la; -no, -na; **— to us no-lo,
no-la; — to him lho, lha; — to them
lho, lha; — to me mo, ma; in — nêle,
nela

January janeiro *m*
John João
Joseph José
**just: to have — acabar de; had —
acabava de

key chave *f.*
kind (to) bom, boa (para)
know saber; conhecer; **to — how** saber

lady senhora *f.*
large grande
last passado -a; **— night** ontem à noite
late *adv.* tarde
lately ùltimamente
laugh rir; **to — at** rir de
learn aprender
leave partir, ir-se embora
left esquerdo -a
less menos
lesson lição *f.*
let permitir; **— us** vamos
letter carta *f.*
library biblioteca *f.*
lie mentira *f.*
light luz *f.*; lâmpada *f.*
like (to) gostar de
Lisbon Lisboa *f.*
listen to escutar

little pouco -a; *adv.* pouco
live morar
loaf of bread pão *m.*
long for ter saudades de
longer: no — já não, não . . . mais
look parecer; to — for procurar
lunch almôço *m.*

maid criada *f.*
man homem *m.*
many muitos -as; how — quantos -as
married casado -a; to get — casar(-se)
Mary Maria
me me; mim; to — me, a mim; it to — mo, ma; them to — mos, mas; with — comigo
mean querer dizer
mend consertar
minute minuto *m.*
miss perder; ter saudades de
money dinheiro *m.*
month mês *m.*
more mais
morning manhã *f.*; — paper jornal da manhã; tomorrow — àmanhã de manhã
mother mãe *f.*
move mover; (*change residence*) mudar-se
much muito; very — muitíssimo; so — tanto; too — demais, demasiado
must dever
my meu, minha
myself me

name nome *m.*
narrow estreito -a
near perto (de)
necessary preciso -a
necktie gravata *f.*
need precisar de
never nunca
new novo -a
news notícia *f.*
newspaper jornal *m.*
New York Nova York
next próximo -a; — door vizinho -a; — week na próxima semana

night noite *f.*; last — ontem à noite
ninth nono -a; (*in dates*) nove
nine nove; — o'clock as nove
no não; — one ninguém; — longer já não
not não; — any não . . . nenhum
nothing nada; não . . . nada
notion: to have a — to estar com vontade de, ter vontade de
now agora, já, logo

o'clock: it is . . . o'clock são as . . .
of de; — the do, da, dos, das; — a dum, duma
off *see* take
old vélho -a; how — is . . . ? quantos anos tem . . . ?; to be . . . years — ter . . . anos
on em, sôbre; to put — vestir, pôr
once uma vez; at — imediatamente, logo, já
one um, uma; — o'clock uma (hora); no — ninguém
only apenas; não . . . senão
open abrir; *adj.* aberto -a
order mandar
other outro -a; each — um ao outro, uns aos outros; nos, se
our nosso -a; ours nosso -a
ourselves nos
out: to put — apagar
owe dever

package pacote *m.*
paper papel *m.*; (*newspaper*) jornal *m.*; morning — jornal da manhã
past (*in telling time*) e
pay pagar
pencil lápis *m.*
permit permitir
person pessoa *f.*
Philadelphia Filadélfia *f.*
place pôr
please faz favor de
pocket algibeira *f.*
polite cortês
poor pobre
poorly mal

Portuguese português, portuguesa
possible possível; **as soon as** — quanto
   antes
press prelo *m.*; **in** — no prelo
pretty lindo -a; — **early** cedinho
professor lente *m.*, professor *m.*
pronounce pronunciar
pronunciation pronúncia *f.*
proof prova *f.*
provided contanto que
pupil aluno *m.*
put pôr; **to** — **on** vestir, pôr; **to** — **out**
   apagar

quarter quarto *m.*
question pregunta *f.*; **to ask a** — fazer
   uma pregunta
quickly ràpidamente

rain chover
read ler
ready pronto; **to get** — **to** preparar-se a
   or para
remember (to) lembrar-se de
rent alugar
repair consertar
repeat repetir
resemble parecer-se com
return voltar
right direito -a; — **away** imediatamente,
   logo
Rio de Janeiro o Rio (de Janeiro) *m.*
road estrada *f.*
roll: to call the — fazer a chamada
room quarto *m.*, sala *f.*
run into dar com

Saturday sábado
say dizer
school escola *f.*
seashore beira-mar *f.*, praia *f.*
seated sentado -a
second segundo -a
secret segrêdo *m.*
see ver
send enviar; — **for** mandar chamar
sentence frase *f.*
shave barbear

she ela
shirt camisa *f.*
shoe sapato *m.*
shopping: to go — ir às compras; (ir)
   fazer compras (*Brazilian*)
show mostrar
shut fechar
side lado *m.*; **on . . . side** de . . . lado
silent: to be — calar-se
simple simples
sing cantar
sir senhor *m.*
sister irmã *f.*
six seis
sleep sono *m.*; **to** — dormir; **to go to** —
   adormecer
sleepy: to be — ter sono
slowly de-vagar
small pequeno -a
smoke fumar
so assim; tão; — **much** tanto; — **that**
   para que, a-fim que
some algum, alguma
sometimes algumas vezes
soon em breve; **as** — **as** assim que, logo
   que; **as** — **as possible** quanto antes
sorry: to be — ter pena, sentir
sound som *m.*
Spanish espanhol
speak falar
spend passar, gastar
station estação *f.*
stay ficar
still ainda
store loja *f.*
story história *f.*
straight *adv.* direito
street rua *f.*
streetcar carro eléctrico *m.*; bonde *m.*
   (*Brazilian*)
strike dar
student aluno *m.*
studious aplicado -a
study estudar
suit fato *m.*; terno *m.* (*Brazilian*); **bathing** — fato de banho *m.*; roupa de
   banho *f.* (*Brazilian*); **to** — parecer
Sunday domingo *m.*

sure certo -a
surprise surpreender; **I am surprised** surpreende-me
sweet doce

table mesa *f.*
take levar, tomar; **to — away** levar; **to — off** tirar; **to — tea** tomar chá; **to — a walk** dar um passeio
talk falar
tall alto -a
tea chá *m.*
teach ensinar
tell dizer
ten dez
tenth décimo -a; (*in dates*) dez
than que, do que; (*before numerals*) de
thanks obrigado -a; **many —** muito obrigado -a
that *conj. and relative pron.* que; **so —** para que, a-fim que; *demonstrative pron.* êsse, essa; isso; aquêle, aquela; aquilo; **of —** dêsse, dessa; disso; daquêle, daquela; daquilo; **in —** nêsse, nessa, nisso; naquêle, naquela, naquilo; **— one** êsse, essa, aquêle, aquela
the o, a, os, as; **of —** do, da, dos, das; **to —** ao, à, aos, às; **in** *or* **on —** no, na, nos, nas; **by —** pelo, pela, pelos, pelas
theater teatro *m.*
their seu, sua; o . . . dêles, o . . . delas
them os, as; -los, -las; -nos, -nas; **to —** lhes; a êles, a elas; **it to —** lho, lha; **— to us** no-los, no-las; **— to — lhos,** lhas; **— to me** mos, mas
themselves se
there aí, ali, lá; **— is, — are** há
these êstes, estas; **of —** dêstes, destas; **in —** nêstes, nestas
they êles, elas
think crer, acreditar, pensar; **to — not** crer que não
thirsty: to be — estar com sêde, ter sêde
thirty trinta; meia
thirty-one trinta-e-um -a

this êste, esta; isto; **of —** dêste, desta; disto; **in —** nêste, nesta; nisto; **— one** êste, esta
those êsses, essas; aquêles, aquelas; os, as; **of —** dêsses, dessas; daquêles, daquelas
three três
Thursday quinta *f.*, quinta-feira *f.*
ticket bilhete *m.*
time tempo *m.*; **it is — to** é tempo de; **what — is it?** que horas são?; **to have the — to** ter tempo para
tired cansado -a; **to get — of** cansar-se de
to a; para; **— the** ao, à, aos, às; (*in telling time*) menos
today hoje
together juntos -as
tomorrow àmanhã; **— morning** àmanhã de manhã
too também; **— much** demais, demasiado
towards para
train combóio *m.*; trem *m.* (*Brazilian*)
travel viajar
trolley car carro eléctrico *m.*; bonde *m.* (*Brazilian*)
true: it is — é verdade
truth verdade *f.*
Tuesday têrça *f.*, têrça-feira *f.*
twelve doze; **— o'clock** meio-dia *m.*, meia-noite *f.*
twenty vinte
two dois, duas

umbrella guarda-chuva *m.*
understand perceber, compreender
United States Estados Unidos *m. pl.*
unkind (to) mau, má (para)
unless a menos que
unmarried solteiro -a
unoccupied vago -a
up: to come — subir; **to get —** levantar-se; **to go —** subir
us nos; nós; **to —** nos, a nós; **it to —** no-lo, no-la; **them to —** no-los, no-las; **with —** connosco
useful útil

very muito
violin violino *m.*
voice voz *f.*

wait esperar
waiter criado *m.*; garçon *m.* (*Brazilian*)
walk passeio *m.*; **to take a —** dar um passeio
want desejar, querer
water água *f.*
way: which — ? por onde?; **that—**por ali
we nós
weather tempo *m.*; **how is the —** ? que tempo faz?; **the — is fine** faz bom tempo; **the — is bad** faz mau tempo
Wednesday quarta *f.*, quarta-feira *f.*
week semana *f.*, oito dias; **next —** na próxima semana
well bem
what que, qual, o que
when quando
where onde, para onde; **from —** donde
whether se; si (*Brazilian*)
which qual; **— way?** por onde?
while enquanto (que), ao passo que
who que, quem
whom que, quem
whose de quem
why porquê

window janela *f.*
wine vinho *m.*
winter inverno *m.*
wish desejar, querer
with com; **— me** comigo; **— you** consigo, com o senhor; **— us** connosco; **— him** consigo, com êle; **— them** consigo, com êles
without *prep.* sem; *conj.* sem que; **to do —** passar sem
word palavra *f.*
work trabalhar; trabalho *m.*
workdays dias úteis
worse pior
worth: to be — valer
write escrever

year ano *m.*; **to be . . . years old** ter . . . anos
yes sim
yesterday ontem
yet ainda; **not —** ainda não
you o senhor, a senhora, a senhorita (*Brazilian*), Vossa Excelência, você; o, a, os, as; si; **to —** lhe, lhes, ao senhor; **with —** consigo, com o senhor
young jovem, novo -a
your seu, sua; o . . . do senhor
yourself, yourselves se

Index

Numbers refer to sections. See Portuguese-English Vocabulary for further references.

167

A CATALOG OF SELECTED
DOVER BOOKS
IN ALL FIELDS OF INTEREST

A CATALOG OF SELECTED DOVER
BOOKS IN ALL FIELDS OF INTEREST

THE ART NOUVEAU STYLE, edited by Roberta Waddell. 579 rare photographs of works in jewelry, metalwork, glass, ceramics, textiles, architecture and furniture by 175 artists—Mucha, Seguy, Lalique, Tiffany, many others. 288pp. 8⅜ × 11¼.
23515-7 Pa. $9.95

AMERICAN COUNTRY HOUSES OF THE GILDED AGE (Sheldon's "Artistic Country-Seats"), A. Lewis. All of Sheldon's fascinating and historically important photographs and plans. New text by Arnold Lewis. Approx. 200 illustrations. 128pp. 9⅜ × 12¼.
24301-X Pa. $7.95

THE WAY WE LIVE NOW, Anthony Trollope. Trollope's late masterpiece, marks shift to bitter satire. Character Melmotte "his greatest villain." Reproduced from original edition with 40 illustrations. 416pp. 6⅛ × 9¼.
24360-5 Pa. $7.95

BENCHLEY LOST AND FOUND, Robert Benchley. Finest humor from early 30's, about pet peeves, child psychologists, post office and others. Mostly unavailable elsewhere. 73 illustrations by Peter Arno and others. 183pp. 5⅜ × 8½.
22410-4 Pa. $3.50

ISOMETRIC PERSPECTIVE DESIGNS AND HOW TO CREATE THEM, John Locke. Isometric perspective is the picture of an object adrift in imaginary space. 75 mindboggling designs. 52pp. 8¼ × 11.
24123-8 Pa. $2.75

PERSPECTIVE FOR ARTISTS, Rex Vicat Cole. Depth, perspective of sky and sea, shadows, much more, not usually covered. 391 diagrams, 81 reproductions of drawings and paintings. 279pp. 5⅜ × 8½.
22487-2 Pa. $4.00

MOVIE-STAR PORTRAITS OF THE FORTIES, edited by John Kobal. 163 glamor, studio photos of 106 stars of the 1940s: Rita Hayworth, Ava Gardner, Marlon Brando, Clark Gable, many more. 176pp. 8⅜ × 11¼.
23546-7 Pa. $6.95

STARS OF THE BROADWAY STAGE, 1940-1967, Fred Fehl. Marlon Brando, Uta Hagen, John Kerr, John Gielgud, Jessica Tandy in great shows—*South Pacific, Galileo, West Side Story*, more. 240 black-and-white photos. 144pp. 8⅜ × 11¼.
24398-2 Pa. $8.95

ILLUSTRATED DICTIONARY OF HISTORIC ARCHITECTURE, edited by Cyril M. Harris. Extraordinary compendium of clear, concise definitions for over 5000 important architectural terms complemented by over 2000 line drawings. 592pp. 7½ × 9⅜.
24444-X Pa. $14.95

THE EARLY WORK OF FRANK LLOYD WRIGHT, F.L. Wright. 207 rare photos of Oak Park period, first great buildings: Unity Temple, Dana house, Larkin factory. Complete photos of Wasmuth edition. New Introduction. 160pp. 8⅜ × 11¼.
24381-8 Pa. $7.95

LIVING MY LIFE, Emma Goldman. Candid, no holds barred account by foremost American anarchist: her own life, anarchist movement, famous contemporaries, ideas and their impact. 944pp. 5⅜ × 8½. 22543-7, 22544-5 Pa., Two-vol. set $13.00

UNDERSTANDING THERMODYNAMICS, H.C. Van Ness. Clear, lucid treatment of first and second laws of thermodynamics. Excellent supplement to basic textbook in undergraduate science or engineering class. 103pp. 5⅜ × 8.
63277-6 Pa. $5.50

TOLL HOUSE TRIED AND TRUE RECIPES, Ruth Graves Wakefield. Popovers, veal and ham loaf, baked beans, much more from the famous Mass. restaurant. Nearly 700 recipes. 376pp. 5⅜ × 8½. 23560-2 Pa. $4.95

FAVORITE CHRISTMAS CAROLS, selected and arranged by Charles J.F. Cofone. Title, music, first verse and refrain of 34 traditional carols in handsome calligraphy; also subsequent verses and other information in type. 79pp. 8⅜ × 11. 20445-6 Pa. $3.50

CAMERA WORK: A PICTORIAL GUIDE, Alfred Stieglitz. All 559 illustrations from most important periodical in history of art photography. Reduced in size but still clear, in strict chronological order, with complete captions. 176pp. 8⅜ × 11¼. 23591-2 Pa. $6.95

FAVORITE SONGS OF THE NINETIES, edited by Robert Fremont. 88 favorites: "Ta-Ra-Ra-Boom-De-Aye," "The Band Played On," "Bird in a Gilded Cage," etc. 401pp. 9 × 12. 21536-9 Pa. $12.95

STRING FIGURES AND HOW TO MAKE THEM, Caroline F. Jayne. Fullest, clearest instructions on string figures from around world: Eskimo, Navajo, Lapp, Europe, more. Cat's cradle, moving spear, lightning, stars. 950 illustrations. 407pp. 5⅜ × 8½. 20152-X Pa. $5.95

LIFE IN ANCIENT EGYPT, Adolf Erman. Detailed older account, with much not in more recent books: domestic life, religion, magic, medicine, commerce, and whatever else needed for complete picture. Many illustrations. 597pp. 5⅜ × 8½. 22632-8 Pa. $7.95

ANCIENT EGYPT: ITS CULTURE AND HISTORY, J.E. Manchip White. From pre-dynastics through Ptolemies: scoiety, history, political structure, religion, daily life, literature, cultural heritage. 48 plates. 217pp. 5⅜ × 8½. (EBE) 22548-8 Pa. $4.95

KEPT IN THE DARK, Anthony Trollope. Unusual short novel about Victorian morality and abnormal psychology by the great English author. Probably the first American publication. Frontispiece by Sir John Millais. 92pp. 6½ × 9¼. 23609-9 Pa. $2.95

MAN AND WIFE, Wilkie Collins. Nineteenth-century master launches an attack on out-moded Scottish marital laws and Victorian cult of athleticism. Artfully plotted. 35 illustrations. 239pp. 6⅛ × 9¼. 24451-2 Pa. $5.95

RELATIVITY AND COMMON SENSE, Herman Bondi. Radically reoriented presentation of Einstein's Special Theory and one of most valuable popular accounts available. 60 illustrations. 177pp. 5⅜ × 8. (EUK) 24021-5 Pa. $3.95

THE EGYPTIAN BOOK OF THE DEAD, E.A. Wallis Budge. Complete reproduction of Ani's papyrus, finest ever found. Full hieroglyphic text, interlinear transliteration, word-for-word translation, smooth translation. 533pp. 6½ × 9¼. (USO) 21866-X Pa. $8.95

COUNTRY AND SUBURBAN HOMES OF THE PRAIRIE SCHOOL PERIOD, H.V. von Holst. Over 400 photographs floor plans, elevations, detailed drawings (exteriors and interiors) for over 100 structures. Text. Important primary source. 128pp. 8⅜ × 11¼. 24373-7 Pa. $5.95

REASON IN ART, George Santayana. Renowned philosopher's provocative, seminal treatment of basis of art in instinct and experience. Volume Four of *The Life of Reason*. 230pp. 5⅜ × 8.　　　　　　　　　　　　24358-3 Pa. $4.50

LANGUAGE, TRUTH AND LOGIC, Alfred J. Ayer. Famous, clear introduction to Vienna, Cambridge schools of Logical Positivism. Role of philosophy, elimination of metaphysics, nature of analysis, etc. 160pp. 5⅜ × 8½. (USCO)
　　　　　　　　　　　　　　　　　　　　　　20010-8 Pa. $2.75

BASIC ELECTRONICS, U.S. Bureau of Naval Personnel. Electron tubes, circuits, antennas, AM, FM, and CW transmission and receiving, etc. 560 illustrations. 567pp. 6½ × 9¼.　　　　　　　　　　　　　　　21076-6 Pa. $8.95

THE ART DECO STYLE, edited by Theodore Menten. Furniture, jewelry, metalwork, ceramics, fabrics, lighting fixtures, interior decors, exteriors, graphics from pure French sources. Over 400 photographs. 183pp. 8⅜ × 11¼.
　　　　　　　　　　　　　　　　　　　　　　22824-X Pa. $6.95

THE FOUR BOOKS OF ARCHITECTURE, Andrea Palladio. 16th-century classic covers classical architectural remains, Renaissance revivals, classical orders, etc. 1738 Ware English edition. 216 plates. 110pp. of text. 9½ × 12¾.
　　　　　　　　　　　　　　　　　　　　　　21308-0 Pa. $11.50

THE WIT AND HUMOR OF OSCAR WILDE, edited by Alvin Redman. More than 1000 ripostes, paradoxes, wisecracks: Work is the curse of the drinking classes, I can resist everything except temptations, etc. 258pp. 5⅜ × 8½. (USCO)
　　　　　　　　　　　　　　　　　　　　　　20602-5 Pa. $3.95

THE DEVIL'S DICTIONARY, Ambrose Bierce. Barbed, bitter, brilliant witticisms in the form of a dictionary. Best, most ferocious satire America has produced. 145pp. 5⅜ × 8½.　　　　　　　　　　　　　20487-1 Pa. $2.50

ERTÉ'S FASHION DESIGNS, Erté. 210 black-and-white inventions from *Harper's Bazar*, 1918-32, plus 8pp. full-color covers. Captions. 88pp. 9 × 12.
　　　　　　　　　　　　　　　　　　　　　　24203-X Pa. $6.50

ERTÉ GRAPHICS, Erté. Collection of striking color graphics: *Seasons, Alphabet, Numerals, Aces* and *Precious Stones*. 50 plates, including 4 on covers. 48pp. 9⅜ × 12¼.　　　　　　　　　　　　　　　　23580-7 Pa. $6.95

PAPER FOLDING FOR BEGINNERS, William D. Murray and Francis J. Rigney. Clearest book for making origami sail boats, roosters, frogs that move legs, etc. 40 projects. More than 275 illustrations. 94pp. 5⅜ × 8½.　　20713-7 Pa. $2.25

ORIGAMI FOR THE ENTHUSIAST, John Montroll. Fish, ostrich, peacock, squirrel, rhinoceros, Pegasus, 19 other intricate subjects. Instructions. Diagrams. 128pp. 9 × 12.　　　　　　　　　　　　　　　23799-0 Pa. $4.95

CROCHETING NOVELTY POT HOLDERS, edited by Linda Macho. 64 useful, whimsical pot holders feature kitchen themes, animals, flowers, other novelties. Surprisingly easy to crochet. Complete instructions. 48pp. 8¼ × 11.
　　　　　　　　　　　　　　　　　　　　　　24296-X Pa. $1.95

CROCHETING DOILIES, edited by Rita Weiss. Irish Crochet, Jewel, Star Wheel, Vanity Fair and more. Also luncheon and console sets, runners and centerpieces. 51 illustrations. 48pp. 8¼ × 11.　　　　　　　　　　23424-X Pa. $2.50

THE RIME OF THE ANCIENT MARINER, Gustave Doré, S.T. Coleridge. Doré's finest work, 34 plates capture moods, subtleties of poem. Full text. 77pp. 9¼ × 12.
22305-1 Pa. $4.95

SONGS OF INNOCENCE, William Blake. The first and most popular of Blake's famous "Illuminated Books," in a facsimile edition reproducing all 31 brightly colored plates. Additional printed text of each poem. 64pp. 5¼ × 7.
22764-2 Pa. $3.50

AN INTRODUCTION TO INFORMATION THEORY, J.R. Pierce. Second (1980) edition of most impressive non-technical account available. Encoding, entropy, noisy channel, related areas, etc. 320pp. 5⅜ × 8½.
24061-4 Pa. $4.95

THE DIVINE PROPORTION: A STUDY IN MATHEMATICAL BEAUTY, H.E. Huntley. "Divine proportion" or "golden ratio" in poetry, Pascal's triangle, philosophy, psychology, music, mathematical figures, etc. Excellent bridge between science and art. 58 figures. 185pp. 5⅜ × 8½.
22254-3 Pa. $3.95

THE DOVER NEW YORK WALKING GUIDE: From the Battery to Wall Street, Mary J. Shapiro. Superb inexpensive guide to historic buildings and locales in lower Manhattan: Trinity Church, Bowling Green, more. Complete Text; maps. 36 illustrations. 48pp. 3⅞ × 9¼.
24225-0 Pa. $2.50

NEW YORK THEN AND NOW, Edward B. Watson, Edmund V. Gillon, Jr. 83 important Manhattan sites: on facing pages early photographs (1875-1925) and 1976 photos by Gillon. 172 illustrations. 171pp. 9¼ × 10.
23361-8 Pa. $7.95

HISTORIC COSTUME IN PICTURES, Braun & Schneider. Over 1450 costumed figures from dawn of civilization to end of 19th century. English captions. 125 plates. 256pp. 8⅜ × 11¼.
23150-X Pa. $7.50

VICTORIAN AND EDWARDIAN FASHION: A Photographic Survey, Alison Gernsheim. First fashion history completely illustrated by contemporary photographs. Full text plus 235 photos, 1840-1914, in which many celebrities appear. 240pp. 6½ × 9¼.
24205-6 Pa. $6.00

CHARTED CHRISTMAS DESIGNS FOR COUNTED CROSS-STITCH AND OTHER NEEDLECRAFTS, Lindberg Press. Charted designs for 45 beautiful needlecraft projects with many yuletide and wintertime motifs. 48pp. 8¼ × 11.
24356-7 Pa. $2.50

101 FOLK DESIGNS FOR COUNTED CROSS-STITCH AND OTHER NEEDLE-CRAFTS, Carter Houck. 101 authentic charted folk designs in a wide array of lovely representations with many suggestions for effective use. 48pp. 8¼ × 11.
24369-9 Pa. $2.25

FIVE ACRES AND INDEPENDENCE, Maurice G. Kains. Great back-to-the-land classic explains basics of self-sufficient farming. The one book to get. 95 illustrations. 397pp. 5⅜ × 8½.
20974-1 Pa. $4.95

A MODERN HERBAL, Margaret Grieve. Much the fullest, most exact, most useful compilation of herbal material. Gigantic alphabetical encyclopedia, from aconite to zedoary, gives botanical information, medical properties, folklore, economic uses, and much else. Indispensable to serious reader. 161 illustrations. 888pp. 6½ × 9¼. (Available in U.S. only)
22798-7, 22799-5 Pa., Two-vol. set $16.45

JAPANESE DESIGN MOTIFS, Matsuya Co. Mon, or heraldic designs. Over 4000 typical, beautiful designs: birds, animals, flowers, swords, fans, geometrics; all beautifully stylized. 213pp. 11⅜ × 8¼. 22874-6 Pa. $7.95

THE TALE OF BENJAMIN BUNNY, Beatrix Potter. Peter Rabbit's cousin coaxes him back into Mr. McGregor's garden for a whole new set of adventures. All 27 full-color illustrations. 59pp. 4¼ × 5½. (Available in U.S. only) 21102-9 Pa. $1.75

THE TALE OF PETER RABBIT AND OTHER FAVORITE STORIES BOXED SET, Beatrix Potter. Seven of Beatrix Potter's best-loved tales including Peter Rabbit in a specially designed, durable boxed set. 4¼ × 5½. Total of 447pp. 158 color illustrations. (Available in U.S. only) 23903-9 Pa. $10.80

PRACTICAL MENTAL MAGIC, Theodore Annemann. Nearly 200 astonishing feats of mental magic revealed in step-by-step detail. Complete advice on staging, patter, etc. Illustrated. 320pp. 5⅜ × 8½. 24426-1 Pa. $5.95

CELEBRATED CASES OF JUDGE DEE (DEE GOONG AN), translated by Robert Van Gulik. Authentic 18th-century Chinese detective novel; Dee and associates solve three interlocked cases. Led to van Gulik's own stories with same characters. Extensive introduction. 9 illustrations. 237pp. 5⅜ × 8½. 23337-5 Pa. $4.50

CUT & FOLD EXTRATERRESTRIAL INVADERS THAT FLY, M. Grater. Stage your own lilliputian space battles. By following the step-by-step instructions and explanatory diagrams you can launch 22 full-color fliers into space. 36pp. 8¼ × 11. 24478-4 Pa. $2.95

CUT & ASSEMBLE VICTORIAN HOUSES, Edmund V. Gillon, Jr. Printed in full color on heavy cardboard stock, 4 authentic Victorian houses in H-O scale: Italian-style Villa, Octagon, Second Empire, Stick Style. 48pp. 9¼ × 12¼. 23849-0 Pa. $3.95

BEST SCIENCE FICTION STORIES OF H.G. WELLS, H.G. Wells. Full novel *The Invisible Man,* plus 17 short stories: "The Crystal Egg," "Aepyornis Island," "The Strange Orchid," etc. 303pp. 5⅜ × 8½. (Available in U.S. only) 21531-8 Pa. $4.95

TRADEMARK DESIGNS OF THE WORLD, Yusaku Kamekura. A lavish collection of nearly 700 trademarks, the work of Wright, Loewy, Klee, Binder, hundreds of others. 160pp. 8¾ × 8. (Available in U.S. only) 24191-2 Pa. $5.95

THE ARTIST'S AND CRAFTSMAN'S GUIDE TO REDUCING, ENLARGING AND TRANSFERRING DESIGNS, Rita Weiss. Discover, reduce, enlarge, transfer designs from any objects to any craft project. 12pp. plus 16 sheets special graph paper. 8¼ × 11. 24142-4 Pa. $3.50

TREASURY OF JAPANESE DESIGNS AND MOTIFS FOR ARTISTS AND CRAFTSMEN, edited by Carol Belanger Grafton. Indispensable collection of 360 traditional Japanese designs and motifs redrawn in clean, crisp black-and-white, copyright-free illustrations. 96pp. 8¼ × 11. 24435-0 Pa. $3.95

SOURCE BOOK OF MEDICAL HISTORY, edited by Logan Clendening, M.D. Original accounts ranging from Ancient Egypt and Greece to discovery of X-rays: Galen, Pasteur, Lavoisier, Harvey, Parkinson, others. 685pp. 5⅜ × 8½.
20621-1 Pa. $10.95

THE ROSE AND THE KEY, J.S. Lefanu. Superb mystery novel from Irish master. Dark doings among an ancient and aristocratic English family. Well-drawn characters; capital suspense. Introduction by N. Donaldson. 448pp. 5⅜ × 8½.
24377-X Pa. $6.95

SOUTH WIND, Norman Douglas. Witty, elegant novel of ideas set on languorous Meditterranean island of Nepenthe. Elegant prose, glittering epigrams, mordant satire. 1917 masterpiece. 416pp. 5⅜ × 8½. (Available in U.S. only)
24361-3 Pa. $5.95

RUSSELL'S CIVIL WAR PHOTOGRAPHS, Capt. A.J. Russell. 116 rare Civil War Photos: Bull Run, Virginia campaigns, bridges, railroads, Richmond, Lincoln's funeral car. Many never seen before. Captions. 128pp. 9⅜ × 12¼.
24283-8 Pa. $6.95

PHOTOGRAPHS BY MAN RAY: 105 Works, 1920-1934. Nudes, still lifes, landscapes, women's faces, celebrity portraits (Dali, Matisse, Picasso, others), rayographs. Reprinted from rare gravure edition. 128pp. 9⅜ × 12¼. (Available in U.S. only) 23842-3 Pa. $7.95

STAR NAMES: THEIR LORE AND MEANING, Richard H. Allen. Star names, the zodiac, constellations: folklore and literature associated with heavens. The basic book of its field, fascinating reading. 563pp. 5⅜ × 8½. 21079-0 Pa. $7.95

BURNHAM'S CELESTIAL HANDBOOK, Robert Burnham, Jr. Thorough guide to the stars beyond our solar system. Exhaustive treatment. Alphabetical by constellation: Andromeda to Cetus in Vol. 1; Chamaeleon to Orion in Vol. 2; and Pavo to Vulpecula in Vol. 3. Hundreds of illustrations. Index in Vol. 3. 2000pp. 6⅛ × 9¼. 23567-X, 23568-8, 23673-0 Pa. Three-vol. set $36.85

THE ART NOUVEAU STYLE BOOK OF ALPHONSE MUCHA, Alphonse Mucha. All 72 plates from *Documents Decoratifs* in original color. Stunning, essential work of Art Nouveau. 80pp. 9⅜ × 12¼. 24044-4 Pa. $7.95

DESIGNS BY ERTE; FASHION DRAWINGS AND ILLUSTRATIONS FROM "HARPER'S BAZAR," Erte. 310 fabulous line drawings and 14 *Harper's Bazar* covers, 8 in full color. Erte's exotic temptresses with tassels, fur muffs, long trains, coifs, more. 129pp. 9⅜ × 12¼. 23397-9 Pa. $6.95

HISTORY OF STRENGTH OF MATERIALS, Stephen P. Timoshenko. Excellent historical survey of the strength of materials with many references to the theories of elasticity and structure. 245 figures. 452pp. 5⅜ × 8½. 61187-6 Pa. $8.95

Prices subject to change without notice.

Available at your book dealer or write for free catalog to Dept. GI, Dover Publications, Inc., 31 East 2nd St. Mineola, N.Y. 11501. Dover publishes more than 175 books each year on science, elementary and advanced mathematics, biology, music, art, literary history, social sciences and other areas.